THE
AMERICAN
REVOLUTION

Other books in the
Interpreting Primary Documents series:

THE
AMERICAN
REVOLUTION

INTERPRETING PRIMARY DOCUMENTS

Charles W. Carey, Book Editor

Daniel Leone, President
Bonnie Szumski, Publisher
Scott Barbour, Managing Editor

GREENHAVEN
PRESS ®

THOMSON
—★—™
GALE

973.3
AME

San Diego • Detroit • New York • San Francisco • Cleveland
New Haven, Conn. • Waterville, Maine • London • Munich

LIBRARY OF CONGRESS CATALOGING-IN-PUBLICATION DATA

The American Revolution / Charles W. Carey, book editor.
    p. cm. — (Interpreting primary documents)
Includes bibliographical references (p.) and index.
ISBN 0-7377-2260-6 (lib. bdg. : alk. paper) —
ISBN 0-7377-2261-4 (pbk. : alk. paper)
    1. United States—History—Revolution, 1775–1783—Sources. I. Carey, Charles W. II. Series.
E203.A5725 2004
973.3—dc21
                                          2003048331

CONTENTS

cally occupying the length and breadth of the rebellious colonies, which far exceeded Great Britain in area. The British prime minister declares that "you cannot conquer America" and calls on Parliament to petition the king for peace.

army were poorly fed, clothed, sheltered, and paid. Private Joseph Plumb Martin describes the conditions in which George Washington's army lived in the days leading up to and during its stay in and around Valley Forge, Pennsylvania, during the winter of 1777–1778.

to sweep across New Jersey, cross the Delaware River, and capture Philadelphia. In this selection, a woman with loyalist sympathies describes her fear of both the Hessian troops and the patriot militias sent to impede their advance.

Chapter 4: Completing the Revolution

president of the United States, believed that the Articles of Confederation gave too little power to the federal government. In this selection from a 1785 letter to James Monroe, he argues in favor of amending the articles to give Congress the power to regulate foreign trade.

FOREWORD

In a debate on the nature of the historian's task, the Canadian intellectual Michael Ignatieff wrote, "I don't think history is a lesson in patriotism. It should be a lesson in truth. And the truth is both painful and many-sided." Part of Ignatieff's point was that those who seek to understand the past should guard against letting prejudice or patriotism interfere with the truth. This point, although simple, is subtle. Everyone would agree that patriotism is no excuse for outright fabrication, and that prejudice should never induce a historian to deliberately lie or deceive. Ignatieff's concern, however, was not so much with deliberate falsification as it was with the way prejudice and patriotism can lead to selective perception, which can skew the judgment of even those who are sincere in their efforts to understand the past. The truth, especially about the how and why of historical events, is seldom simple, and those who wish to genuinely understand the past must be sensitive to its complexities.

Each of the anthologies in the Greenhaven Press Interpreting Primary Documents series strives to portray the events and attitudes of the past in all their complexity. Rather than providing a simple narrative of the events, each volume presents a variety of views on the issues and events under discussion and encourages the student to confront and examine the complexity that attends the genuine study of history.

Furthermore, instead of aiming simply to transmit information from historian to student, the series is designed to develop and train students to become historians themselves, by focusing on the interpretation of primary documents. Such documents, including newspaper articles, speeches, personal reflections, letters, diaries, memoranda, and official reports, are the raw material from which the historian refines an authentic understanding of the past. The anthology examining desegregation, for instance, includes the voices of presidents, state governors, and ordinary citizens, and draws from the *Congressional Record,* newspapers and magazines, letters, and books published at the time. The selections differ in scope and opinion as well, allowing the student to examine the issue of desegregation from a variety of perspectives. By looking frankly at the arguments offered by those in favor of racial segregation and by those opposed, for example, students can better understand those arguments, the people who advanced them, and the time in which they lived.

The structure of each book in the Interpreting Primary Documents series helps readers sharpen the critical faculties the serious study of history requires. A concise introduction outlines the era or event at hand and provides the necessary historical background. The chapters themselves begin with a preface containing a straightforward account of the events discussed and an overview of how these events can be interpreted in different ways by examining the different documents in the chapter. The selections, in turn, are chosen for their accessibility and relevance, and each is preceded by a short introduction offering historical context and a summary of the author's point of view. A set of questions to guide interpretation accompanies each article and encourages readers to examine the authors' prejudices, probe their assumptions, and compare and contrast the various perspectives offered in the chapter. Finally, a detailed timeline traces the development of key events, a comprehensive bibliography of selected secondary material guides further research, and a thorough index lets the reader quickly access relevant information.

As Ignatieff remarked, in the same debate in which he urged the historian to favor truth over blind patriotism, "History for me is the study of arguments." The Interpreting Primary Documents series is for readers eager to understand the arguments, and attitudes, that animated historical change.

INTRODUCTION

The American Revolution is one of the most important events in the history of the world. The United States grew to become one of the most, if not the most, powerful countries in the world. Its founding documents, the Declaration of Independence and the U.S. Constitution, have served as models for governments all over the world.

American schoolchildren are taught routinely that the American Revolution occurred because the tyrannous British insisted on trampling upon the rights of virtuous Americans. A better explanation is that war broke out between the Americans and the British because both held tenaciously to different theories of political ideas. In other words, the American Revolution was not so much a struggle between tyranny and virtue as it was a struggle between competing theories of how the British Empire should be governed.

The British believed that Parliament had the power to legislate for the British Empire in all affairs. But for approximately one hundred years—from the mid–seventeenth century to the mid–eighteenth century—Parliament had mostly ignored the American colonies because Great Britain was faced with bigger problems at home and in Europe. During this period, Americans had developed their colonial assemblies into legislative bodies that were quite competent to handle local affairs. By 1756 Americans had come to believe that Parliament should legislate only for matters that concerned the empire as a whole, whereas local affairs should be handled by the colonial assemblies. The inability of each side to understand the other's point of view eventually led to war.

British Ideas About Government

Perhaps the most sacred idea the British held about government was the supremacy of Parliament. Although the king or queen of England was universally acknowledged as the supreme ruler of Great Britain, the monarch's ability to rule effectively depended on his or her ability to get along with Parliament. In Parliament, representatives of the British ruling class met to consider proposals from the monarch, which were written by the royal ministers or cabinet members. These proposals were not routinely endorsed but were sometimes subjected to intense scrutiny and rigorous debate; many were amended, and some were rejected outright. The working relationship was similar to the one that exists today between the president of the United States, working through the cabinet, and the U.S. Congress.

In order to vote for a member of Parliament, one had to possess a considerable amount of landed property. This meant that only the wealthiest British landowners played a role in government. Most men and all women were barred from voting in parliamentary elections; surprisingly, the lack of the franchise seemed to matter little to most of them.

Regional assemblies did not exist in England, so Parliament made decisions or legislated matters on a local scale as well as for imperial and national affairs. All legislation, including that passed by colonial assemblies, had to be approved by the monarch—usually after being reviewed by the royal ministers—and by Parliament before it went into effect.

American Ideas About Government

For the most part, colonial Americans did not object to having the proceedings of their colonial assemblies reviewed by Parliament or the royal ministers. Americans considered themselves to be loyal subjects of the British Empire and were almost universally loyal to the king. Prior to the Stamp Act crisis, most of them acknowledged the supremacy of Parliament as well. For example, few Americans objected to the Navigation Acts, which prohibited Americans from trading directly with non-British merchants, mostly because the acts also protected American merchants from foreign competition in their trade with other British possessions. However, most Americans also believed in the supremacy of the colonial assemblies within their colonies. Unlike the British, Americans played a major role in their own local government by voting for and serving in their colonial assemblies. Property requirements existed in the colonies just as they did in England, but property was so much easier to acquire in America that the majority of free male colonists were able to vote.

Between the founding of the first American colonies during the early 1600s and the Stamp Act crisis during the 1760s, Americans developed a unique political system that can best be described as "split sovereignty." Parliament regulated external affairs, such as trade and foreign diplomacy, whereas the colonial assemblies regulated internal affairs, such as the operation of the courts and the raising of the militias. The British tolerated split sovereignty until the 1760s, mostly because their preoccupation with European affairs led them to ignore the colonies. This situation changed after the French and Indian War, when the British refocused their attention on America.

"No Taxation Without Representation"

The first major step toward the American Revolution was taken in 1765, when Parliament, at the urging of King George III's ministers, passed the Stamp Act. This act required that all documents, legal or otherwise, be stamped. The act was similar to one already in force in England, except that the fees were actually higher in England than in America.

The purpose of the Stamp Act was to raise revenue for the British treasury in the American colonies. Great Britain had just finished fighting the Seven Years' War (known in America as the French and Indian War), and the war debt was astronomical. Much of the debt had been incurred while fighting the French in America. Since the British believed that their victory removed the threat of a French invasion of the American colonies, they thought it reasonable to expect the colonists to defray their fair share of the war debt.

To the surprise of the British, the Americans felt otherwise. First, Americans did not think that part of the war debt was theirs to pay; they had never feared a French invasion to begin with, they had gained no land or trade concessions as a result of the victory, and they had contributed men and money to the fighting, just as the British had. Secondly, and more importantly, the Stamp Act had been passed without consulting Americans. Since it interfered with their internal affairs, Americans could not accept it because it usurped the power of their assemblies. At the Stamp Act Congress in 1765, colonial delegates rejected the Stamp Act on the grounds that it taxed them illegally. Their argument was that they were not represented in Parliament, and therefore Parliament could not tax them.

"No taxation without representation" became the American rallying cry, and groups such as the Sons of Liberty began organizing opposition to the act. Citizens and merchants were encouraged to participate in an embargo of British imports. Most stamp agents were intimidated into giving up their positions; those who did serve were tarred and feathered. Within a year, Parliament repealed the Stamp Act; however, it insisted that it did indeed have the authority to tax the colonies in whatever way it desired.

Virtual Representation

The British were stumped by the American response to the Stamp Act, and during the Stamp Act crisis they sought a way to respond to "no taxation without representation." They eventually developed the theory of "virtual representation," which declared that Americans were as well represented in Parliament as any other British subjects. Fewer than 5 percent of the males living in the British Isles could vote, but the other 95 percent (and their women and children, as well as British subjects in Canada, India, and the other colonies) were looked after by Parliament nonetheless. The British argued sincerely that Parliament did not represent the interests of the British ruling class only, but that it also took into consideration the best interests of the entire British Empire before making decisions.

Virtual representation struck the Americans as absurd.

From their own experiences in the colonial assemblies, they knew full well that politicians advance their own self-interests while believing sincerely that they do so for the good of the whole. In order for the rights of everyone to be protected, they insisted, everyone must have a voice in the political proceedings that concern them.

Independence Versus Reconciliation

The Stamp Act crisis ended in 1766, but the debate over colonial rights continued. Parliament passed other acts designed to raise revenue in the American colonies, but every time the Americans objected that Parliament had no right to tax them. Americans responded by resorting to nonimportation and to mob intimidation of British officials and agents. British troops were stationed in the major cities to maintain law and order, but their presence led instead to violence and bloodshed. In 1770 fighting between civilians and troops broke out in Boston and in New York City.

The situation came to a head in 1773. Angry colonists protested the provisions of the Tea Act by dumping tons of tea into Boston Harbor. The British response to the Boston Tea Party was swift and harsh. Parliament, again at the urging of the king's ministers, closed Boston Harbor and disbanded the Massachusetts colonial government. Rather than cow Americans, these actions served only to galvanize them into action. Committees of correspondence were organized to keep the various colonies advised of breaking news. In 1774 the First Continental Congress met as a way for the colonies to gain redress for their grievances. But the British showed little interest in discussing or understanding the American political theory of split sovereignty; to the British, the idea that Parliament was supreme in all areas except the internal affairs of the colonies was absurd.

In 1775 Americans seemed to be of two minds about breaking away from Great Britain. Many still revered the king, even though they had come to despise Parliament and the king's ministers. Whereas orators such as Patrick Henry spoke out forcefully for liberty, others spoke out just as

This 1774 British print depicts a tax collector being tarred and feathered by several patriots, while the Boston Tea Party occurs in the background.

forcefully for reconciliation. American protests and petitions to the king's ministers, Parliament, and British residents explaining the American point of view fell mostly on deaf ears. When fighting broke out in April 1775, many colonists who subscribed to American political theory renounced the violence and called for reconciliation by sending King George III the so-called Olive Branch Petition. The petition begged him to rein in his ministers and influence Parliament to arrive at a peaceful solution to the problem. But when the king rejected the petition and declared America to be in a state of rebellion, it served only to propel Americans further along the road to independence.

Having failed to convince Great Britain of the merit of split sovereignty, the choice remained either to submit meekly to parliamentary rule or to fight for full independence.

Obstacles to Winning the War

When war finally broke out, it was not clear that either side would be able to win easily. Major obstacles were faced by both sides. One big problem was how to mobilize or neutralize loyalists, slaves, and Indians. The other big problem was how to recruit, supply, maintain, and transport armies and navies.

Loyalists presented problems to both Americans and the British. John Adams estimated that as many as one-third of all Americans remained loyal to the Crown, and suppressing them was high on the list of priorities for the patriots. Patriot militias made it their business to identify and harass loyalists in their communities, and more than eighty thousand loyalists were either killed or forced to evacuate. Nevertheless, more than fifteen thousand loyalists joined the British army, and some of the fiercest fighting of the war was waged between the patriot and loyalist militias. In this sense, the American Revolution was as much a civil war as a war for independence.

For the British, the loyalist problem involved how to protect loyalists and how to recruit more of them into the ranks. There simply were not enough British troops to protect every loyalist, especially in the backcountry, and a great many loyalists who might have fought for their king remained neutral or even became lukewarm patriots as a means of self-preservation. From the beginning of the war, but especially after the British defeat at Saratoga, part of the British war strategy involved recruiting more loyalists. This desire was a major factor in shifting the war to the South, which was presumed to be full of loyalists.

As with loyalists, so with slaves. Approximately one-third of the South's residents and a significant percentage of the ones in New York and Pennsylvania were in bondage for life, and keeping the slaves in line while the masters were off at war was a major concern for Americans. The British endeavored to recruit slaves to fight under the royal standard by promising them their freedom (toward the end of the war, the Americans would try the same tactic). For the most part, slaves played a minor role in the actual conflict; their presence, however, greatly influenced the strategy of both sides.

In colonial times, the British had established strong trading ties with a number of Indians, especially the Iroquois in the north and the Cherokee and Creek in the south. During the war, all three attacked American settlers on the western frontier. Major massacres, of Americans against Indians and vice versa, took place in western New York and Pennsylvania. Keeping the Indians under control was a major distraction for patriot militias, and recruiting more Indians to fight for the king was an ongoing problem for the British.

Military Problems Facing the British

In 1775 the British had one of the finest armies in the world. However, the Royal Army also had the responsibility of defending British possessions around the globe. The threat of invasion by their European enemies, especially the French, prevented the British from committing all of their troops against the upstart Americans. This problem was solved partially by signing treaties with several German princes, who provided thousands of soldiers to serve alongside British regulars. Thousands more were recruited from the ranks of American loyalists. In the end, though, the British were never able to put as many men into the field as they needed.

When war broke out, the Royal Navy was also one of the world's best. And yet, like the British army, it was hard-pressed to protect British dominions around the world, so it could never concentrate its resources against the Americans. Outside New York City, the fleet lacked docks and ports where it could stop for repairs and supplies. Major repairs could only be obtained in Halifax, Nova Scotia, and in the Caribbean, both of which were too far from the scene to make them effective. Blockading the entire American coast proved to be impossible due to the lack of small, fast ships, which the Americans possessed in great numbers.

A third military problem for the British was how to conquer the vast expanse that was America. Taken together, the thirteen rebellious colonies were larger than the British Isles. Good roads were a rarity in America, so the only way to travel from one end to the other was by ship. To make matters worse, America was thousands of miles from Great Britain, and troops, ships, and supplies from the homeland had to cross the Atlantic Ocean. Then, too, the terrain of America was something with which British troops had little experience. Their battlefield tactics were geared for fighting in open fields, not forested hills. Also, the terrain made for good cover for patriot ambushes of small British units traveling cross country or foraging for food or fodder.

Military Problems Facing the Americans

The Americans were in worse shape than the British: They entered the war with no standing army at all. At first they relied on the state militias to provide officers and men for the Continental army. The militias performed well when suppressing loyalists and harassing British troop movements through their states, but their lack of professional military training kept them from fighting effectively against the British on the battlefield. Later the Americans tried to create a standing army via short-term enlistments and cash bonuses. The result was that the Continental army was always full of raw recruits, usually drawn from the ranks of the poor and unemployed instead of battle-hardened veterans.

The problem of supplying the Continental army was never satisfactorily solved either. The French were eager to avenge their defeat at the hands of the British during the French and Indian War, and they provided the Americans with much of the weapons, ammunition, artillery, and other supplies their army needed. After the American victory at Saratoga, the French also provided the Americans with the services of a French army and navy, without which the Americans could not have won the war. However, throughout the war, Congress was hard-pressed to keep the army fed and clothed, and when the army took up winter quarters it always lacked proper shelter. Whereas the British navy was stretched thin, the Americans possessed no navy at all. Although Congress managed to scrape together a small one, it spent most of the war blockaded in Narragansett Bay. One solution to this problem was privateers, privately owned vessels fitted out with cannon and licensed by Congress to prey on British shipping. Privateers proved to be very effective against British trade, but they were no match for the ships of the Royal Navy. Not until the French entered the war did the Americans have a fleet to rival the British.

Ironically, a major obstacle to financing the war for the Americans was the political ideals for which they were fighting. Unwilling to submit to the will of Parliament in terms of taxation and other internal affairs, the states also refused to submit to the will of the Continental Congress. As a result, Congress became more a steering committee than a national government, especially since the states refused to grant it the power to tax. Even after the Articles of Confederation, in effect the first U.S. Constitution, were ratified, Congress could do no more than ask the states politely for money to fund the war.

Not being able to tax, Congress did the only other thing it could: print paper money. By the end of the war, more than $250 million in Continental dollars had been put into circulation. Meanwhile, the individual states were financing their part of the war effort in the same way, and no one knows exactly how much paper money the thirteen states printed. The result was economic chaos. By war's end, Continental dollars were worthless. Army quartermasters could not get citizens to "sell" their flour or cattle, so they were forced to seize them, leaving the former owner with an IOU.

The problem of finances was solved in part by the generosity of France and the Netherlands. The Dutch loaned the Americans millions of dollars with which to purchase weapons, ammunition, and other supplies, mostly because they looked forward to trading directly with an America freed from the restrictions of the Navigation Acts.

Terrain posed a problem for the Americans as well. Because of the lack of roads, and the fact that the British controlled major stretches of the Atlantic coastline for a considerable portion of the time, transportation and communication among the various states was extremely difficult.

The War: 1775

The War of the American Revolution began in 1775, almost fifteen months before independence was formally declared. The first battle took place in New England in April when British troops marched to Lexington, Massachusetts, and Concord, New Hampshire, to seize patriot powder and ammunition. On their way back to Boston, the British were ambushed by thousands of patriots and suffered heavy casualties. Two months later, a patriot army of more than ten thousand was attacked by the British at the Battle

General George Washington takes command of the Continental army in July 1775. The army relied largely on volunteers to fill its ranks.

of Bunker Hill; the inexperienced patriots inflicted heavy losses on the British before being forced to retreat. In July General George Washington took command of the makeshift American army in the name of the Continental Congress. Little else happened on this front until the following March, when Washington's Continental army captured Dorchester Heights overlooking Boston, thus forcing the British to evacuate.

Meanwhile, fighting took place to the north and south of Boston. In September 1775 an American force invaded Canada in hopes of getting the Canadians to join the rebellion; it almost captured Quebec before being forced to retreat the following year. In December a British force consisting of regular troops, white loyalists, and runaway slaves was defeated by Virginia militiamen at the Battle of Great Bridge, thus removing the possibility that Virginia could be used as a base of operations for the Royal Army and Navy.

The War: 1776

Two days before the Declaration of Independence was signed, a British army under General William Howe landed at Staten Island in New York. Over the next few months, Howe routed Washington's Continentals on Long Island and Manhattan Island and easily captured New York City. Then he chased Washington's army as it retreated across New Jersey into Pennsylvania while dispatching a small force to capture Newport, Rhode Island. Howe's victories almost brought the war to a close, but Washington managed to keep a few thousand troops in the field. In late December, the Continentals attacked the Hessian garrison at Trenton, New Jersey, capturing or killing about one thousand enemy troops. For the next several days, Washington led British general Charles Cornwallis on a merry chase, defeating another British garrison at Princeton before going into winter quarters in the hills around Morristown, New Jersey. Washington's victories were meaningless from a military point of view because the British quickly recaptured both Trenton and Princeton; however, they were indispensable from a morale point of view and did much to keep the spirit of revolution alive.

Although most of the fighting in 1776 took place between New York City and Philadelphia, several significant engagements took place elsewhere. The royal governor of North Carolina had convinced the British ministry that most of the residents of his colony were loyal to the Crown, so the Royal Army and Navy embarked on the so-called Southern Expedition. The expedition was held up for a number of reasons; still, it reached the Carolina coast before Howe began operations in New York. But before it could arrive, fourteen hundred loyalists who were on their way to join the expedition were routed by a patriot militia in February at the Battle of Moore's Creek. No more loyalists were forthcoming, so the expedition sailed on to Charleston, South Carolina. In June, having failed to take the city, the expedition sailed to New York to join Howe. A patriot army under the command of Benedict Arnold held up a British advance from Canada long enough to make the British retire northward for the winter, and patriot militias held off several Indian attacks along the western frontiers.

The War: 1777

Having established himself in New York City, Howe next decided to capture Philadelphia, the largest city in America and the seat of the Continental Congress. For reasons known only to himself, Howe chose not to advance on Philadelphia by land across New Jersey or by sea by sailing up the Delaware River; instead, he sailed to the head of Chesapeake Bay and marched overland from there, thus wasting most of the year's fighting season. In September he easily outmaneuvered Washington at the Battle of Brandywine Creek and entered Philadelphia a few days later. In October Washington attempted to oust Howe but was defeated soundly at the Battle of Germantown. With Howe in firm control of the city, Washington took up winter quarters at nearby Valley Forge.

Despite the loss of Philadelphia, 1777 was a good year

for America. To the north, another British army was advancing from Canada, this time under the command of General John Burgoyne. Burgoyne had grievously underestimated the difficulty with which his army would advance through the upstate New York wilderness as well as the ability of the patriots to frustrate his efforts to supply his army. In October, after almost a month of heavy fighting near the village of Saratoga, Burgoyne surrendered his surrounded army to American general Horatio Gates.

The War: 1778

Burgoyne's defeat was a major victory for the Americans because it allowed the French to enter the war openly against the British. While the French made plans to invade southern England, a French fleet and army arrived in America in July. After threatening to free New York City from British occupation, the French force joined part of Washington's army in an assault on Newport, Rhode Island. Poor communication between the two forces contributed to the failure of their attack.

Meanwhile, Howe had been replaced as British commander in chief by General Henry Clinton. Clinton realized that the French entrance into the war made New York City vulnerable, so in June he evacuated Philadelphia and began the long march back to New York City. En route he was attacked by the Continental army at Monmouth, New Jersey; the fighting was indecisive, and the British returned to New York City in time to deter the French from attacking.

Most of the fighting of the first two years had taken place between Boston and Philadelphia. Having achieved little in this region, in 1778 the British turned their attention once again to the South. Although the Southern Expedition of 1776 had failed, the British ministry had always believed that many southern loyalists and disaffected slaves would join a British force campaigning in the South. Making use of these loyalists and slaves would free up many British soldiers and ships to defend the British Isles against a French invasion. Leaving behind a small force to defend

New York City, in December Clinton attacked and captured Savannah, Georgia.

The western front was quite active during 1778. The Indian allies of the British continued to threaten frontier settlements, and they massacred settlers in Pennsylvania's Wyoming Valley and New York's Cherry Valley. At the same

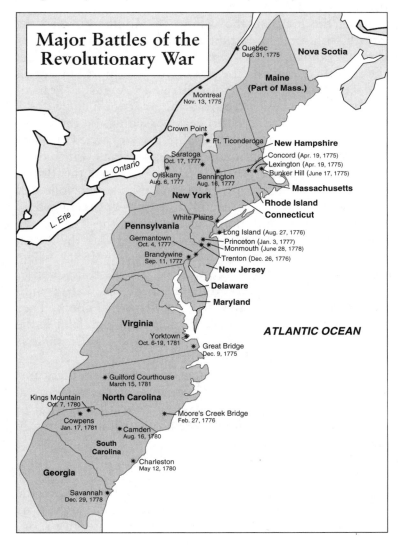

Major Battles of the Revolutionary War

Quebec Dec. 31, 1775

Nova Scotia

Maine (Part of Mass.)

Montreal Nov. 13, 1775

Crown Point

Ft. Ticonderoga

L. Ontario

Saratoga Oct. 17, 1777

Oriskany Aug. 6, 1777

Bennington Aug. 16, 1777

New Hampshire

Concord (Apr. 19, 1775)
Lexington (Apr. 19, 1775)
Bunker Hill (June 17, 1775)

Massachusetts

New York

L. Erie

White Plains

Rhode Island

Connecticut

Pennsylvania

Germantown Oct. 4, 1777

Brandywine Sep. 11, 1777

Long Island (Aug. 27, 1776)
Princeton (Jan. 3, 1777)
Monmouth (June 28, 1778)
Trenton (Dec. 26, 1776)

New Jersey

Delaware

Maryland

Virginia

ATLANTIC OCEAN

Yorktown Oct. 6-19, 1781

Great Bridge Dec. 9, 1775

Guilford Courthouse March 15, 1781

Kings Mountain Oct. 7, 1780

North Carolina

Cowpens Jan. 17, 1781

Camden Aug. 16, 1780

Moore's Creek Bridge Feb. 27, 1776

South Carolina

Charleston May 12, 1780

Georgia

Savannah Dec. 29, 1778

time, a small band of Virginians commanded by George Rogers Clark captured Kaskaskia in the Old Northwest and began to assert American control over that region. Clark completed his conquest of the region the following February by capturing Vincennes.

The War: 1779

Shifting the focus of the war to the South provided the British with some important victories in 1779. Having captured Savannah, British forces were able to sweep through the rest of Georgia. By the end of the year, most of Georgia had been restored to royal control. In August a Franco-American force besieged Savannah, but it was unable to expel the British, who inflicted heavy casualties on the allies.

Meanwhile, British and loyalist troops carried the war into other parts of the South. Although a small British force was repulsed at Port Royal, South Carolina, the British mounted a successful invasion of Virginia. Norfolk and Portsmouth were burned, and Royal Navy vessels raided up the major rivers and along both sides of the Chesapeake Bay. Ironically, most of the loyalists serving with the British were from New York, Pennsylvania, and New Jersey, where the British military presence was the strongest. Few southern loyalists or slaves joined these expeditions. Patriot militias in the South kept the slave population in check. They also kept many loyalists from fighting, although later in the war partisan warfare between patriot and loyalist militias would plague the southern backcountry.

The year had only two bright spots for the Americans. One was the capture of two minor forts on the outskirts of New York City. The other was the British evacuation of Newport, which was done to reinforce Clinton's army in the South.

The War: 1780

The southern strategy continued to pay dividends to the British in 1780. Clinton captured Charleston, South Carolina, in May, in the process taking more than five thousand Continental troops as his prisoners. He then dispatched General Charles Cornwallis to conquer the rest of South Carolina. To oppose Cornwallis, Congress sent Horatio Gates, the victor at Saratoga. Gates quickly threw together the Southern Army, but in June it was completely destroyed by Cornwallis at the Battle of Camden, South Carolina. After pacifying eastern South Carolina, in September Cornwallis invaded North Carolina.

It began to appear that the southern strategy would soon result in the British conquest of the entire South, if not all of America. But the Americans began to bounce back in October, when General Nathanael Greene, Gates's replacement, defeated a British force of regulars and loyalists at Kings Mountain, North Carolina. Greene's victory exposed Cornwallis's flank, and the British were forced to return to South Carolina for the rest of the year.

The War: 1781

The southern strategy completely fell to pieces during 1781. In January the British suffered another major defeat at the Battle of Cowpens, North Carolina. Buoyed by the victory, Greene marched into South Carolina in an effort to reclaim that state. He was soon pursued by Cornwallis, who chased Greene fruitlessly all the way into north-central North Carolina. Greene finally gave battle at Guilford Courthouse, and although he was driven from the field, his troops inflicted heavy casualties on the British. By now it was clear that the vast numbers of southern loyalists and slaves whom the British had been counting on to fight for the king either did not exist or would not be forthcoming. Short on men and supplies, Cornwallis decided to retire from North Carolina.

Meanwhile, Virginia had been invaded by the British again, and Cornwallis decided to join up with the invaders at Yorktown. Upon learning of Cornwallis's plans, General George Washington immediately made plans to trap the British army on the narrow peninsula where Yorktown sits. He convinced French admiral F.J.P. de Grasse to blockade

Chesapeake Bay, thus preventing Cornwallis's escape or relief. Then Washington and French general Comte de Rochambeau combined their troops and marched from the outskirts of New York City to Yorktown. Cornwallis found himself outnumbered by more than 2 to 1, and after several weeks of desultory fighting, he surrendered his command to Washington.

The War: 1782–1783

The war did not end at Yorktown, even though Parliament voted to discontinue hostilities once it received word of Cornwallis's surrender. Loyalist and patriot militias continued to fight one another, especially in the southern backcountry, while the British Indian allies continued to pose a threat to the frontier. Also, three major American cities remained in British hands.

In April 1782 Clinton was replaced by General Guy Carleton. In less than two months he evacuated Charleston and Savannah and began planning the evacuation of New York City. In November a tentative peace treaty was arranged, which was confirmed in September 1783. One month later the British left New York City, thus bringing the war to an end.

Creating State Governments

Having broken away from Great Britain, the Americans had also to establish a new government. This process began in 1775, continued throughout the war, and did not end until 1791, when the Bill of Rights was ratified. Throughout the process, Americans struggled to implement the political theory of split sovereignty over which they had split with the British.

The Battles of Lexington and Concord prompted the thirteen colonies to begin establishing state governments. In June 1775 Massachusetts altered its colonial charter by replacing the royal governor with an executive council. By the time the Declaration of Independence was signed, four more states—New Hampshire, South Carolina, Virginia, and New Jersey—had written new constitutions. Virginia's was, by far, the most far-reaching. Whereas the other constitutions were compromise works between those who favored independence and those who favored reconciliation, the first Virginia constitution established a state government that was beholden to no greater power. Not surprisingly, this constitution, and the bill of rights that preceded it, served as models for other state constitutions and for the U.S. Constitution.

Generally speaking, the state constitutions reflected the Americans' long-standing theories of local government. Most power was retained by the legislatures. Since royal governors had treated the colonial assemblies contemptuously, in many cases disbanding an assembly that refused to give in to a governor's demands, most state governors were reduced to figurehead status. Pennsylvania even dispensed with a governor altogether, establishing instead an executive council. The judicial branches were essentially made a part of the legislatures, as they had been during colonial times.

The Continental Congress

While the states were establishing their own governments, the Continental Congress struggled to assert its authority over the states. In fact, it was never able to do so. At the time of its creation in 1774, the Congress was not intended to serve as the ruling body of the United States. Instead, it was intended to serve as a steering committee, to guide the activities of the states in their conflict with Great Britain. The various states sent delegates to represent themselves in Congress, but no one pretended that Congress had the power to rule over the states. Odd as this may seem, it was perfectly consistent with the notion of government that Americans had at the time, that the state legislatures were the supreme authorities within their own boundaries, and that a national legislature, be it Parliament or Congress, had only the authority to control external affairs, such as trade and foreign diplomacy. Congress had the power to request aid from the various states, but it did not have the power to coerce a state to obey its dictates. For all practical purposes, Americans had no national government during the early days of the American Revolution.

The Articles of Confederation

By 1776 it had become clear that Americans needed some sort of formal national government in order to weld them together as a more effective military coalition. That same year Congress began writing the Articles of Confederation, mostly for the purpose of presenting a united front to the European nations that the Americans hoped to attract as allies. The articles brought the states together in a federal union; although most powers were reserved for the states, some, like the power to wage war and conduct foreign diplomacy, were reserved for Congress. Under the articles, Congress did not possess the power to tax, raise troops, or regulate commerce; these were all left within the purview of the states.

In 1777 the final draft of the Articles of Confederation was completed and sent to the states for ratification. Although most states signed on almost immediately, three of the smaller states held off, mostly because they feared the power that the articles gave to the national government. Weak as the articles were, they presented a threat to states that, at that very moment, were fighting a difficult war to free themselves from a strong national government. Not until 1781, just a few months before the British surrender at Yorktown brought major hostilities to an end, were the articles sufficiently amended to satisfy those states that feared national government.

The U.S. Constitution

For eight years (1781–1789) the Articles of Confederation served as the instrument of government for the United States. For many people, the articles provided a perfectly satisfactory form of government. Although Congress served as a unifying force for the nation, most power remained vested in the states. This situation was exactly what the patriots intended to establish in the mid-1770s when they rebelled against Great Britain.

For many other Americans, however, the articles were woefully deficient. Many of the leading patriots, including James Madison and Alexander Hamilton, had become nationalists during the American Revolution, and they believed the articles prevented the United States from becoming a strong and powerful nation. For those engaged in mercantile activity, the articles presented major drawbacks to the conduct of international and interstate commerce. As part of the British Empire, American merchants had enjoyed the protection of the Royal Navy as well as favored status within the empire under the Navigation Acts. The articles, however, prevented the United States from keeping a navy in peacetime, thus putting American shipping at the mercy of pirates, most notably the Barbary pirates of the Mediterranean. The articles also prevented Congress from regulating interstate trade and severely restricted its power to negotiate trade treaties with foreign governments that were binding in every respect on the states. While under British rule, Americans had been protected to a certain degree from Indians living to the west. With the British gone from the Old Northwest under the terms of the Treaty of Paris, no force remained to keep the Indians in check, especially since the articles prohibited the national government from keeping a standing army.

Several attempts were made to amend the articles, but none succeeded. This was because the articles could not be amended without unanimous approval of the states, and at least one state always objected to the amendment under consideration. Frustrated with the national government's inability to play a more active role, a number of leading men from the various states called for a convention to be held in Philadelphia in 1787 "to render the constitution of the Federal Government adequate to the exigencies of the Union," as Hamilton put it.

Once the convention began, the doors were locked and no official notes were taken. Most delegates had come with the idea of replacing, not amending, the Articles of Confederation, but to do so openly would have constituted plotting the overthrow of the government. After several months the delegates hammered out a document that implemented split sovereignty; it provided for a strong national government, but it also reserved a number of important powers to the states. This document, the U.S. Constitution, was submitted to the states for ratification that same year.

Ratifying the Constitution

It surprises twenty-first-century Americans to discover that eighteenth-century Americans were not unanimously in favor of the Constitution. But having just won a war for independence, many refused to consider implementing the same sort of government they had just fought to get rid of. The debate for and against ratification went on for almost a year, with men of considerable stature arguing on both sides. The Constitution was ratified in 1788 and went into effect the following year, but many Americans did not feel truly comfortable with the government it created until ratification of the first ten amendments, known more popularly as the Bill of Rights, in 1791. The Bill of Rights promised to protect Americans from intrusion by the national government on the basic rights that many had perceived the British to have trampled upon during the crises of the 1760s and the 1770s.

The adoption of the Bill of Rights marked the completion of the American Revolution. After a struggle of almost thirty years, Americans now had the form of government, split sovereignty, which they had wanted for years. The national government was responsible for external affairs, and the state governments were left in charge of their own internal affairs. Each provided a check against the other so that the rights and livelihoods of the citizenry would be protected. Although future changes would be made to American government, most notably the abolition of slavery and the enfranchisement of women, all were made within the framework of the Constitution.

1

THE DEBATE OVER COLONIAL RIGHTS

CHAPTER PREFACE

The American Revolution was precipitated by the Stamp Act crisis. Passed by Parliament in 1765, the Stamp Act was intended to help Great Britain pay its debts from the French and Indian War by raising money in the American colonies. Instead, the act provoked howls of protest from the colonists, who insisted that the act was unconstitutional. Most Americans believed that Parliament should control the external affairs of the British Empire while the colonial legislatures should control the internal affairs of the colonies. They did not object to such measures as the Navigation Acts because these acts regulated the empire's trade. However, Americans objected vociferously to the Stamp Act because it raised money by taxing them against their wills.

The Stamp Act Congress of 1765 lodged a formal protest against the Stamp Act on behalf of the colonies. The principal objection was that Americans were not represented in Parliament, hence that body had no right to tax them. This declaration gave rise to the rallying cry "no taxation without representation." To the British, this argument made no sense. Most people in Great Britain could not vote because of property requirements, and yet nonvoters rarely complained. This situation gave rise to the theory of "virtual representation," whereby Parliament was seen as giving equal consideration to the best interests of all imperial subjects.

Virtual representation failed to satisfy the Americans' notion of fairness, no matter how strongly the British tried to urge it upon them. In time, some Americans advanced the notion that the colonies could best redress their grievances by breaking away from Great Britain. By 1775 their cries had become deafening. And yet many other Americans, who were themselves upset by the British government's efforts to tax the colonies, believed that the situation could best be handled by continuing to explain the American point of view to the king and to Parliament.

The Stamp Act Congress Declares "No Taxation Without Representation"

Stamp Act Congress

In March 1765 Parliament passed the so-called Stamp Act. This law sought to raise money by taxing all legal and commercial transactions in the colonies. Any piece of paper, such as a will or a bill of sale, had to be stamped in order to be valid. Similar legislation had been passed by Parliament to cover the king's subjects living in the British Isles, who adhered placidly to its provisions. The act made the court of admiralty in Halifax, Nova Scotia, the final authority in judging violations of the act.

The colonists objected to the act for three major reasons. First, stamps could only be bought with gold or silver, not colonial paper money. Second, the Halifax court was far removed from the thirteen colonies, and cases tried in that court were decided by British judges, not colonial juries. Third, the duties were not intended to regulate trade but to raise revenue, which the colonists believed should be done only by their own colonial assemblies.

Seven months after the Stamp Act was passed, representatives of nine colonies met in New York City. Known as the Stamp Act Congress, this meeting condemned the act and called for its repeal. Five months later, or almost one year to the day that it was passed, the act was indeed repealed, but only after the colonists had demonstrated their strong determination to resist its provisions.

Stamp Act Congress, *Declaration of Rights*, March 1765.

As you read, consider the following questions:
1. To whom is the Declaration of Rights addressed? Why?
2. Other than the three reasons stated above, does the Declaration of Rights offer any other reasons for objecting to the Stamp Act?
3. Does the argument outlined in the Declaration of Rights make sense? If so, why? If not, why not?

The members of this congress, sincerely devoted, with the warmest sentiments of affection and duty to his majesty's person and government, inviolably attached to the present happy establishment of the protestant succession, and with minds deeply impressed by a sense of the present and impending misfortunes of the British colonies on this continent; having considered as maturely as time will permit, the circumstances of the said colonies, esteem it our indispensable duty to make the following declarations of our humble opinion, respecting the most essential rights and liberties of the colonists, and of the grievances under which they labour, by reason of several late acts of parliament.

1. That his majesty's subjects in these colonies, owe the same allegiance to the crown of Great Britain, that is owing from his subjects born within the realm, and all due subordination to that august body the parliament of Great Britain.

2. That his majesty's liege subjects in these colonies, are entitled to all the inherent rights and liberties of his natural born subjects, within the kingdom of Great Britain.

3. That it is inseparably essential to the freedom of a people, and the undoubted right of Englishmen, that no taxes be imposed on them but with their own consent, given personally, or by their representatives.

4. That the people of these colonies are not, and, from their local circumstances, cannot be, represented in the House of Commons in Great Britain.

5. That the only representatives of the people of these colonies, are persons chosen therein by themselves; and

that no taxes ever have been, or can be constitutionally imposed on them, but by their respective legislatures.

6. That all supplies to the crown being free gifts of the people, it is unreasonable and inconsistent with the principles and spirit of the British constitution, for the people of Great Britain to grant to his majesty the property of the colonists.

7. That trial by jury, is the inherent and invaluable right of every British subject in these colonies.

8. That the late act of parliament, entitled, an act for granting and applying certain stamp duties, and other duties, in the British colonies and plantations in America, &c., by imposing taxes on the inhabitants of these colonies, and the said act, and several other acts, by extending the jurisdiction of the courts of admiralty[1] beyond its ancient limits, have a manifest tendency to subvert the rights and liberties of the colonists.

9. That the duties imposed by several late acts of parliament, from the peculiar circumstances of these colonies, will be extremely burdensome and grievous; and from the scarcity of specie,[2] the payment of them absolutely impracticable.

10. That as the profits of the trade of these colonies ultimately center in Great Britain, to pay for the manufactures which they are obliged to take from thence, they eventually contribute very largely to all supplies granted there to the crown.

11. That the restrictions imposed by several late acts of parliament on the trade of these colonies, will render them unable to purchase the manufactures of Great Britain.

12. That the increase, prosperity and happiness of these colonies, depend on the full and free enjoyments of their rights and liberties, and an intercourse with Great Britain

---

1. Courts of admiralty heard cases involving violations of the various acts of Parliament that regulated colonial trade. These courts operated without juries, and they sometimes handed down rather arbitrary decisions. In 1764 a special court of admiralty was established in Halifax, Nova Scotia, and given jurisdiction over all admiralty cases in America.   2. Specie was precious metal (gold and silver), of which there was little in America.

mutually affectionate and advantageous.

13. That it is the right of the British subjects in these colonies, to petition the king, or either house of parliament.

Lastly, That it is the indispensable duty of these colonies, to the best of sovereigns, to the mother country, and to themselves, to endeavour by a loyal and dutiful address to his majesty, and humble applications to both houses of parliament, to procure the repeal of the act for granting and applying certain stamp duties, of all clauses of any other acts of parliament, whereby the jurisdiction of the admiralty is extended as aforesaid, and of the other late acts for the restriction of American commerce.

A Member of Parliament Refutes "No Taxation Without Representation"

Soame Jenyns

The notion that Parliament could not tax the colonies because the colonies were not represented in Parliament made no sense to the British. In order to vote in eighteenth-century England, a man had to own a certain amount of real property, or land. Most Englishmen, perhaps as many as 90 percent, were therefore denied the right to vote. Their number included a great many wealthy merchants and industrialists who owned factories, ships, stocks and bonds, but very little land. Consequently, the newly industrialized sections of England, such as the manufacturing towns of Manchester and Birmingham, were hardly represented in Parliament at all because very few voters lived there. Perhaps most surprisingly (to modern Americans, at least), nonvoters raised very little objection to being disenfranchised.

Soame Jenyns was a member of Parliament and of the Board of Trade and Plantations, the government entity most responsible for colonial affairs. He took particular exception to "no taxation without representation." In 1765 he penned a scathing reply to the resolutions of the Stamp Act Congress, in which he outlines the concept of "virtual representation." According to Jenyns, the best interests of all British subjects, whether they may vote or not, are represented in Parliament, which has the right to tax whomever or whatever it desires.

Soame Jenyns, *The Objections to the Taxation of Our American Colonies by the Legislature of Great Britain, Briefly Consider'd*, London 1765.

As you read, consider the following questions:
1. Jenyns states that "no man . . . is taxed by his own consent." What does he mean? Do you agree or disagree?
   Why?
2. Jenyns argues that colonial charters simply gave coloniz-
   ers the right to incorporate, and did not give colonies the
   right to govern themselves. How does he justify this position? Do you agree or disagree? Why?
3. Which presents the more convincing argument, "The
   Stamp Act Congress Declares 'No Taxation Without
   Representation'" or "A Member of Parliament Refutes
   'No Taxation Without Representation'"? Why?

The right of the legislature of Great Britain to impose taxes
on her American colonies, and the expediency of exerting
that right in the present conjuncture, are propositions so
indisputably clear that I should never have thought it necessary to have undertaken their defense had not many arguments been lately flung out, both in papers and conversation, which with insolence equal to their absurdity deny
them both. As these are usually mixed up with several patriotic and favorite words, such as liberty, property, Englishmen, etc., which are apt to make strong impressions
on that more numerous part of mankind who have ears but
no understanding, it will not, I think, be improper to give
them some answers. . . .

The great capital argument, which I find on this subject,
. . . is this: that no Englishman is or can be taxed but by his
own consent, by which must be meant one of these three
propositions—either that no Englishman can be taxed
without his own consent as an individual; or that no Englishman can be taxed without the consent of the persons
he chooses to represent him; or that no Englishman can be
taxed without the consent of the majority of all those who
are elected by himself and others of his fellow subjects to
represent them. Now, let us impartially consider whether
any of these propositions are in fact true. If not, then this

wonderful structure which has been erected upon them falls at once to the ground, and like another Babel perishes by a confusion of words, which the builders themselves are unable to understand.

First, then, that no Englishman is or can be taxed but by his own consent as an individual: this is so far from being true, that it is the very reverse of truth, for no man that I know of is taxed by his own consent; and an Englishman, I believe, is as little likely to be so taxed as any man in the world.

Second, that no Englishman is or can be taxed but by the consent of those persons whom he has chosen to represent him: for the truth of this I shall appeal only to the candid representatives of those unfortunate counties which produce cider and shall willingly acquiesce under their determination.[1]

Lastly, that no Englishman is or can be taxed without the consent of the majority of those who are elected by himself and others of his fellow subjects to represent them: this is certainly as false as the other two, for every Englishman is taxed, and not one in twenty represented: copyholders, leaseholders, and all men possessed of personal property only, choose no representatives. Manchester, Birmingham, and many more of our richest and most flourishing trading towns send no members to Parliament, consequently cannot consent by their representatives because they choose none to represent them.[2] Yet are they not Englishmen? Or are they not taxed?

I am well aware that I shall hear Locke, Sidney, Selden,[3] and many other great names quoted to prove that every

---

1. In 1765 apple cider was a thriving industry in England's West Country (Devon, Somerset, Gloucestershire, Worcestershire, and Herefordshire). Cider was considered to be the equal of the best French wines among London's society set. It was taxed so heavily that by the end of the eighteenth century the commercial production of cider had virtually ceased.   2. This situation did not change until 1832, when the first Reform Bill was passed.   3. John Locke, Algernon Sidney, and John Selden were seventeenth-century English political writers. Their works were well known to Americans, who often quoted from them while justifying "no taxation without representation."

Englishman, whether he has a right to vote for a representative or not, is still represented in the British Parliament; in which opinion they all agree. On what principle of common sense this opinion is founded I comprehend not, but on the authority of such respectable names I shall acknowledge its truth; but then I will ask one question, and on that I will rest the whole merits of the cause. Why does not this imaginary representation extend to America as well as over the whole island of Great Britain? If it can travel 300 miles, why not 3,000? If it can jump over rivers and mountains, why cannot it sail over the ocean? If the towns of Manchester and Birmingham, sending no representatives to Parliament, are notwithstanding there represented, why are not the cities of Albany and Boston equally represented in that assembly? Are they not alike British subjects? Are they not Englishmen? Or are they only Englishmen when they solicit for protection, but not Englishmen when taxes are required to enable this country to protect them?

But it is urged that the colonies are by their charters placed under distinct governments, each of which has a legislative power within itself, by which alone it ought to be taxed; that if this privilege is once given up, that liberty which every Englishman has a right to is torn from them, they are all slaves, and all is lost.

The liberty of an Englishman is a phrase of so various a signification, having within these few years been used as a synonymous term for blasphemy, bawdy, treason, libels, strong beer, and cider, that I shall not here presume to define its meaning; but I shall venture to assert what it cannot mean; that is, an exemption from taxes imposed by the authority of the Parliament of Great Britain. Nor is there any charter that ever pretended to grant such a privilege to any colony in America; and had they granted it, it could have had no force, their charters being derived from the Crown, and no charter from the Crown can possibly supersede the right of the whole legislature. Their charters are undoubtedly no more than those of all corporations, which empower them to make bylaws and raise duties for the purposes of their own police, forever subject to the superior authority of Parliament. And in some of their charters, the manner of exercising these powers is specified in these express words, "according to the course of other corporations in Great Britain"; and, therefore, they can have no more pretense to plead an exemption from this parliamentary authority than any other corporation in England.

It has been moreover alleged that, though Parliament may have power to impose taxes on the colonies, they have no right to use it because it would be an unjust tax; and no supreme or legislative power can have a right to enact any law in its nature unjust. To this I shall only make this short reply: that if Parliament can impose no taxes but what are equitable, and the persons taxed are to be the judges of that equity, they will in effect have no power to lay any tax at all. No tax can be imposed exactly equal on all, and if it is not equal, it cannot be just; and if it is not just, no power whatever can impose it; by which short syllogism, all taxation is at an end. But why it should not be used by Englishmen on this side of the Atlantic as well as by those on the other I do not comprehend.

A Maryland Lawyer Refutes Virtual Representation

Daniel Dulany

The notion that the American colonies enjoyed virtual representation in Parliament was as absurd to most Americans as the notion of "no taxation without representation" was to most Englishmen. In 1765, most colonists were quite willing to acknowledge the supremacy of Parliament, and cheerfully agreed that Parliament alone had the right to regulate trade, as well as all other external affairs of the British empire. They did not, however, assent to the idea that Parliament's supremacy extended to the internal affairs of the colonies. They particularly disagreed with the idea that Parliament could pass acts designed to raise revenue among the colonists, which the Stamp Act was intended to do. Instead, they avowed that only the colonial assemblies possessed the right to raise revenue via taxation.

Daniel Dulany was a Maryland lawyer who had been trained in law in London. In 1765 he wrote the pamphlet from which these excerpts are taken as a rebuttal to Soame Jenyns's pamphlet, *The Objections to the Taxation of Our American Colonies by the Legislature of Great Britain, Briefly Consider'd*. In it Dulany argued that virtual representation, though it may exist in Great Britain, does not apply to the colonies.

As you read, consider the following questions:
1. Does Dulany's argument that the colonies are not represented virtually in Parliament, while many nonvoting

Daniel Dulany, *Considerations on the Propriety of Imposing Taxes in the British Colonies, for the Purpose of Raising a Revenue, by Act of Parliament*, Annapolis 1765.

Englishmen are, make sense? If so, why? If not, why not?
2. Dulany wrote this selection in rebuttal to Soame Jenyns; if you were Jenyns, how might you rebut Dulany's argument?

In the Constitution of England, the three principal forms of government, monarchy, aristocracy, and democracy, are blended together in certain proportions; but each of these orders, in the exercise of the legislative authority, hath its peculiar department from which the other are excluded. In this division, the granting of supplies or laying taxes is deemed to be the province of the House of Commons, as the representative of the people. All supplies are supposed to flow from their gift; and the other orders are permitted only to assent, or reject generally, not to propose any modification, amendment, or partial alteration of it.

This observation being considered, it will undeniably appear that in framing the late Stamp Act, the Commons acted in the character of representatives of the colonies. They assumed it as the principle of that measure, and the propriety of it must therefore stand or fall as the principle is true or false: for the preamble sets forth that the Commons of Great Britain had resolved to give and grant the several rates and duties imposed by the Act; but what right had the Commons of Great Britain to be thus munificent at the expence of the Commons of America? To give property not belonging to the giver, and without the consent of the owner, is such evident and flagrant injustice in ordinary cases, that few are hardy enough to avow it; and therefore when it really happens, the fact is disguised and varnished over by the most plausible pretences the ingenuity of the giver can suggest. But it is alledged that there is a *virtual*, or *implied representation* of the colonies springing out of the Constitution of the British Government. And it must be confessed on all hands, that as the representation is not actual, it is virtual, or it doth not exist at all; for no third kind of representation can be imagined. The colonies claim the privilege which is common to all British subjects, of being taxed only with their own consent given by their representatives, and all the advocates for the Stamp Act admit this claim. Whether, therefore, upon the whole matter, the imposition of the Stamp Duties is a proper exercise of constitutional authority, or not, depends upon the single question, Whether the commons of Great Britain are virtually the representatives of the commons of America, or not.

The advocates for the Stamp Act admit in express terms, that 'the colonies do not chuse members of Parliament', but they assert that 'the colonies are virtually represented in the same manner with the nonelectors resident in Great Britain'. How have they proved this position? Where have they defined, or precisely explained what they mean by the expression, *virtual representation?*

They argue, that 'the right of election being annexed to certain species of property, to franchises, and inhabitancy in some particular places, a very small part of the land, the property, and the people of England, is comprehended in those descriptions. All landed property not freehold, and all monied property are excluded.[1] The merchants of London, the proprietors of the public funds, the inhabitants of Leeds, Halifax, Birmingham, and Manchester,[2] and that great corporation of the East India Company, none of them chuse their representatives, and yet are they all represented in Parliament, and the colonies being exactly in their situation, are represented in the same manner.'. . .

I shall undertake to disprove the supposed similarity of situation, whence the same kind of representation is deduced of the inhabitants of the colonies, and of the British nonelectors; and, if I succeed, the notion of a virtual representation of the colonies must fail, which, in truth, is a

1. In order to vote in parliamentary elections, a voter had to own outright a certain amount of land. Rented land did not confer voting status on the renter, nor did "monied property," for example, stocks, bonds, or an interest in a factory or some other business concern. 2. These cities had grown from practically nothing as a result of the Industrial Revolution, which began in England around 1750. As their leading citizens were mostly either merchants or the owners of monied property, few people in these cities could vote.

mere cobweb spread to catch the unwary and entangle the weak. I would be understood. I am upon a question of propriety, not of power; and though some may be inclined to think it is to little purpose to discuss the one when the other is irresistible, yet are they different considerations; and, at the same time that I invalidate the claim upon which it is founded, I may very consistently recommend a submission to the law, whilst it endures. . . .

Lessees for years,[3] copyholders, proprietors of the public funds, inhabitants of Birmingham, Leeds, Halifax, and Manchester, merchants of the City of London, or members of the corporation of the East India Company, are, as such, under no personal incapacity to be electors; for they may acquire the right of election, and there are actually not only a considerable number of electors in each of the classes of lessees for years, etc., but in many of them, if not all, even members of Parliament. The interests, therefore, of the nonelectors, the electors, and the representatives are individually the same; to say nothing of the connection among neighbors, friends, and relations. The security of the nonelectors against oppression is that their oppression will fall also upon the electors and the representatives. The one cannot be injured and the other indemnified. Further, if the nonelectors should not be taxed by the British Parliament, they would not be taxed at all; and it would be iniquitous, as well as a solecism in the political system, that they should partake of all the benefits resulting from the imposition and application of taxes, and derive an immunity from the circumstance of not being qualified to vote. Under this constitution, then, a double or virtual representation may be reasonably supposed.

The electors, who are inseparably connected in their interests with the nonelectors, may be justly deemed to be the representatives of the nonelectors, at the same time they exercise their personal privilege in their right of election, and the members chosen, therefore, the representatives of both.

3. renters who have entered into long-term leases for the land they rent

This is the only rational explanation of the expression *virtual representation.* None has been advanced by the assertors of it, and their meaning can only be inferred from the instances by which they endeavor to elucidate it; and no other meaning can be stated to which the instances apply. . . . The inhabitants of the colonies are, as such, incapable of being electors, the privilege of election being exercisable only in person, and, therefore, if every inhabitant of America had the requisite freehold, not one could vote but upon the supposition of his ceasing to be an inhabitant of America and becoming a resident in Great Britain, a supposition which would be impertinent because it shifts the question: Should the colonies not be taxed by parliamentary impositions; their respective legislatures have a regular, adequate, and constitutional authority to tax them; and therefore there would not necessarily be an iniquitous and absurd exemption from their not being represented by the House of Commons? . . .

There is not that intimate and inseparable relation between the electors of Great Britain and the Inhabitants of the colonies, which must inevitably involve both in the same taxation; on the contrary, not a single actual elector in England, might be immediately affected by a taxation in America, or by a statute which would have a general operation and effect upon the properties of the inhabitants of the colonies. The latter might be oppressed in a thousand shapes, without any sympathy, or exciting any alarm in the former. Moreover, even acts, oppressive and injurious to the colonies in an extreme degree, might become popular in England, from the promise or expectation, that the very measures which depressed the colonies, would give ease to the Inhabitants of Great-Britain. It is indeed true, that the interests of England and the colonies are allied, and an injury to the colonies produced into all its consequences, will eventually affect the mother country; yet these consequences being generally remote, are not at once foreseen; they do not immediately alarm the fears, and engage the passions of the English electors; the connection between a freeholder of

Great Britain, and a British American being deductible only through a train of reasoning, which few will take the trouble, or can have opportunity, if they have capacity, to investigate; wherefore the relation between the British Americans, and the English electors, is a knot too infirm to be relied on as a competent security, especially against the force of a present, counteracting expectation of relief.

If it would have been a just conclusion, that the colonies being exactly in the same situation with the nonelectors of England, are therefore represented in the same manner; it ought to be allowed, that the reasoning is solid, which, after having evinced a total dissimilarity of situation, infers that their representation is different.

If the commons of Great Britain have no right by the constitution, to give and grant property not belonging to themselves or others, without their consent actually or virtually given; if the claim of the colonies not to be taxed without their consent, signified by their representatives, is well founded; if it appears that the colonies are not actually represented by the commons of Great Britain, and that the notion of a double or virtual representation, doth not with any propriety apply to the people of America; then the principle of the Stamp Act, must be given up as indefensible on the point of representation.

A Virginia Planter Argues for Independence

Patrick Henry

Despite the repeal of the Stamp Act in 1765, relations between the Americans and the British government continued to deteriorate. Parliament passed more acts intended to raise revenue in the American colonies, and the colonists resisted them just as vigorously as they had the Stamp Act. By March 1775, when Patrick Henry delivered this speech, the British Army had occupied Boston and the battles of Lexington and Concord were less than a month away.

Henry was a Virginia planter who served in the House of Burgesses, the colonial assembly's lower house. He spoke during an unofficial meeting of the Burgesses, which had just been dismissed by Lord Dunmore, Virginia's royal governor. He followed several members who urged the Burgesses to continue to work peacefully for the redress of their grievances. He rejected their arguments and argued instead for independence, even at the cost of war. His remarks were sent by the Virginia Committee of Correspondence to the assemblies of the other colonies, where they inspired others to seek independence as well. The oration became one of the most famous speeches in U.S. history.

As you read, consider the following questions:
1. Why does Henry argue for independence and war rather than a peaceful settlement of colonial grievances? Does his argument make sense?
2. In your opinion, how would the Stamp Act Congress, Soame Jenyns, and Daniel Dulany have reacted to Henry's speech?

Patrick Henry, "Give Me Liberty, or Give Me Death," speech before the House of Burgesses, March 23, 1775.

No man thinks more highly than I do of the patriotism, as well as abilities, of the very worthy gentlemen who have just addressed the House. But different men often see the same subject in different lights; and, therefore, I hope it will not be thought disrespectful to those gentlemen if, entertaining as I do opinions of a character very opposite to theirs, I shall speak forth my sentiments freely and without reserve. This is no time for ceremony. The question before the House is one of awful moment to this country. For my own part, I consider it as nothing less than a question of freedom or slavery; and in proportion to the magnitude of the subject ought to be the freedom of the debate. It is only in this way that we can hope to arrive at truth, and fulfill the great responsibility which we hold to God and our country. Should I keep back my opinions at such a time, through fear of giving offense, I should consider myself as guilty of treason towards my country, and of an act of disloyalty toward the Majesty of Heaven, which I revere above all earthly kings.

Mr. President, it is natural to man to indulge in the illusions of hope. We are apt to shut our eyes against a painful truth, and listen to the song of that siren till she transforms us into beasts. Is this the part of wise men, engaged in a great and arduous struggle for liberty? Are we disposed to be of the number of those who, having eyes, see not, and, having ears, hear not, the things which so nearly concern their temporal salvation? For my part, whatever anguish of spirit it may cost, I am willing to know the whole truth; to know the worst, and to provide for it.

I have but one lamp by which my feet are guided, and that is the lamp of experience. I know of no way of judging of the future but by the past. And judging by the past, I wish to know what there has been in the conduct of the British ministry for the last ten years to justify those hopes with which gentlemen have been pleased to solace themselves and the House. Is it that insidious smile with which our petition has been lately received? Trust it not, sir; it will prove a snare to your feet. Suffer not yourselves to be betrayed with a kiss. Ask yourselves how this gracious reception of our petitions comports with those warlike preparations which cover our waters and darken our land. Are fleets and armies necessary to a work of love and reconciliation? Have we shown ourselves so unwilling to be reconciled that force must be called in to win back our love? Let us not deceive ourselves, sir. These are the implements of war and subjugation; the last arguments to which kings resort. I ask gentlemen, sir, what means this martial array, if its purpose be not to force us to submission? Can gentlemen assign any other possible motive for it? Has Great Britain any enemy, in this quarter of the world, to call for all this accumulation of navies and armies? No, sir, she has none. They are meant for us: they can be meant for no other. They are sent over to bind and rivet upon us those chains which the British ministry have been so long forging. And what have we to oppose to them? Shall we try argument? Sir, we have been trying that for the last ten years. Have we anything new to offer upon the subject? Nothing. We have held

Patrick Henry delivers his "Give Me Liberty, or Give Me Death" speech. The sentiment became the war cry of the American Revolution.

the subject up in every light of which it is capable; but it has been all in vain. Shall we resort to entreaty and humble supplication? What terms shall we find which have not been already exhausted? Let us not, I beseech you, sir, deceive ourselves. Sir, we have done everything that could be done to avert the storm which is now coming on. We have petitioned; we have remonstrated; we have supplicated; we have prostrated ourselves before the throne, and have implored its interposition to arrest the tyrannical hands of the ministry and Parliament. Our petitions have been slighted; our remonstrances have produced additional violence and insult; our supplications have been disregarded; and we have been spurned, with contempt, from the foot of the throne! In vain, after these things, may we indulge the fond hope of peace and reconciliation. There is no longer any room for hope. If we wish to be free—if we mean to preserve inviolate those inestimable privileges for which we have been so long contending—if we mean not basely to abandon the noble struggle in which we have been so long engaged, and which we have pledged ourselves never to abandon until the glorious object of our contest shall be obtained—we must fight! I repeat it, sir, we must fight! An appeal to arms and to the God of hosts is all that is left us!

They tell us, sir, that we are weak; unable to cope with so formidable an adversary. But when shall we be stronger? Will it be the next week, or the next year? Will it be when we are totally disarmed and when a British guard shall be stationed in every house? Shall we gather strength by irresolution and inaction? Shall we acquire the means of effectual resistance by lying supinely on our backs and hugging the delusive phantom of hope, until our enemies shall have bound us hand and foot? Sir, we are not weak if we make a proper use of those means which the God of nature hath placed in our power. The millions of people, armed in the holy cause of liberty, and in such a country as that which we possess, are invincible by any force which our enemy can send against us. Besides, sir, we shall not fight our battles alone. There is a just God who presides over the destinies of nations, and who will raise up friends to fight our battles for us. The battle, sir, is not to the strong alone; it is to the vigilant, the active, the brave. Besides, sir, we have no election. If we were base enough to desire it, it is now too late to retire from the contest. There is no retreat but in submission and slavery! Our chains are forged! Their clanking may be heard on the plains of Boston! The war is inevitable—and let it come! I repeat it, sir, let it come.

It is in vain, sir, to extenuate the matter. Gentlemen may cry, Peace, Peace—but there is no peace. The war is actually begun! The next gale that sweeps from the north will bring to our ears the clash of resounding arms! Our brethren are already in the field! Why stand we here idle? What is it that gentlemen wish? What would they have? Is life so dear, or peace so sweet, as to be purchased at the price of chains and slavery? Forbid it, Almighty God! I know not what course others may take; but as for me, give me liberty or give me death!

A Connecticut Clergyman Argues Against Independence

Samuel Seabury

In 1774 the First Continental Congress met in Philadelphia to discuss how the colonies might win redress of their grievances with Parliament. Elected by the various colonial assemblies, the Congress's delegates voted to establish the Continental Association. The association was intended to persuade Americans to boycott goods made in the British Isles, and membership was supposed to be voluntary. To make sure that the association worked, however, Congress empowered local "committees of inspection" to harass those merchants who did not join and cooperate with the association and to expose their customers to the wrath of public opinion.

Samuel Seabury was an Episcopal minister who was born and raised in Groton, Connecticut. Seabury was appalled by what he considered to be the tyrannical and extralegal manner in which Congress enforced the Continental Association. Under the pen name "A Westchester Farmer," in December 1774 he wrote the pamphlet *A View of the Controversy Between Great Britain and Her Colonies* in response to a pro-Congress pamphlet. In it, Seabury denounces "the mean, paltry, narrow, stupid design of the Congress." He also declares himself in favor of keeping America in the British Empire, and suggests that American grievances might best be redressed by the colonial assemblies petitioning Parliament.

Samuel Seabury, *A View of the Controversy Between Great Britain and Her Colonies, etc., etc.* London 1775.

As you read, consider the following questions:
1. Why does Seabury dislike Congress? Why does he oppose independence, even though he freely admits "that Americans are entitled to freedom"?
2. To what degree does Seabury agree with the ideas expressed in "A Member of Parliament Refutes 'No Taxation Without Representation'"?

I wish you had explicitly declared to the public your ideas of the natural rights of mankind. Man in a state of nature may be considered as perfectly free from all restraints of law and government; and then the weak must submit to the strong. From such a state, I confess, I have a violent aversion. I think the form of government we lately enjoyed a much more eligible state to live in, and cannot help regretting our having lost it by the equity, wisdom, and authority of the Congress, who have introduced in the room of it confusion and violence, where all must submit to the power of a mob.

You have taken some pains to prove what would readily have been granted you—that liberty is a very good thing, and slavery a very bad thing. But then I must think that liberty under a king, Lords, and Commons is as good as liberty under a republican Congress; and that slavery under a republican Congress is as bad, at least, as slavery under a king, Lords, and Commons; and, upon the whole, that liberty under the supreme authority and protection of Great Britain is infinitely preferable to slavery under an American Congress. I will also agree with you "that Americans are entitled to freedom." I will go further: I will own and acknowledge that not only Americans but Africans, Europeans, Asiatics, all men of all countries and degrees, of all sizes and complexions, have a right to as much freedom as is consistent with the security of civil society. And I hope you will not think me an "enemy" to the natural "rights of mankind" because I cannot wish them more. We must, however, remember that more liberty may, without inconvenience, be allowed to individuals in a small government than can be admitted of in a large empire.

But when you assert that "since Americans have not by any act of theirs empowered the British Parliament to make laws for them, it follows they can have no just authority to do it," you advance a position subversive of that dependence which all colonies must, from their very nature, have on the mother country. By the British Parliament, I suppose you mean the supreme legislative authority, the King, Lords, and Commons, because no other authority in England has a right to make laws to bind the kingdom, and consequently no authority to make laws to bind the colonies. In this sense I shall understand and use the phrase "British Parliament."

Now the dependence of the colonies on the mother country has ever been acknowledged. It is an impropriety of speech to talk of an independent colony. The words "independency" and "colony" convey contradictory ideas: much like killing and sparing. As soon as a colony becomes independent on its parent state, it ceases to be any longer a colony; just as when you kill a sheep, you cease to spare him. The British colonies make a part of the British Empire. As parts of the body they must be subject to the general laws of the body. To talk of a colony independent of the mother country is no better sense than to talk of a limb independent of the body to which it belongs.

In every government there must be a supreme, absolute authority lodged somewhere. In arbitrary governments this power is in the monarch: in aristocratical governments, in the nobles; in democratical, in the people or the deputies of their electing. Our own government being a mixture of all these kinds, the supreme authority is vested in the King, nobles, and people; i.e., the King, House of Lords, and House of Commons elected by the people. This supreme authority extends as far as the British dominions extend. To suppose a part of the British dominions which is not subject to the power of the British legislature is no better sense than to suppose a country, at one and the same time, to be and not to be a part of the British dominions. If, therefore, the colony of New York be a part of the British dominions, the colony of New York is subject and dependent on the supreme legislative authority of Great Britain. . . .

The position that we are bound by no laws to which we have not consented, either by ourselves or our representatives, is a novel position, unsupported by any authoritative record of the British constitution, ancient or modern. It is republican in its very nature, and tends to the utter subversion of the English monarchy.

This position has arisen from an artful change of terms. To say that an Englishman is not bound by any laws but those to which the representatives of the nation have given their consent is to say what is true. But to say that an Englishman is bound by no laws but those to which *he* has consented in person, or by *his* representative, is saying what never was true, and never can be true. A great part of the people in England have no vote in the choice of representatives and therefore are governed by laws to which they never consented either by *themselves* or by *their* representatives.

The right of colonists to exercise a legislative power is no natural right. They derive it not from nature but from the indulgence or grant of the parent state, whose subjects they were when the colony was settled, and by whose permission and assistance they made the settlement.

Upon supposition that every English colony enjoyed a legislative power independent of the Parliament; and that the Parliament has no just authority to make laws to bind them, this absurdity will follow: that there is no power in the British Empire which has authority to make laws for the whole Empire, *i.e.*, we have an Empire without government; or, which amounts to the same thing, we have a government which has no supreme power. All our colonies are independent of each other. Suppose them independent of the British Parliament—what power do you leave to govern the whole? None at all. You split and divide the Empire into a number of petty, insignificant states. This is the direct, the necessary tendency of refusing submission to acts of Parliament. Every man who can see one inch beyond his nose must see this consequence. And every man who endeavors to accelerate the independency of the colonies on the British Parliament endeavors to accelerate the ruin of the British Empire.

To talk of being liege subjects to King George while we disavow the authority of Parliament is another piece of Whiggish nonsense. I love my King as well as any Whig in America or England either, and am as ready to yield him all lawful submission. But, while I submit to the King, I submit to the authority of the laws of the state, whose guardian the King is. The difference between a good and a bad subject is only this, that the one obeys, the other transgresses the law. The difference between a loyal subject and a rebel is that the one yields obedience to and faithfully supports the supreme authority of the state, and the other endeavors to overthrow it. If we obey the laws of the King, we obey the laws of the Parliament. If we disown the authority of the Parliament, we disown the authority of the King. There is no medium without ascribing powers to the King which the constitution knows nothing of, without making him superior to the laws and setting him above all restraint. These are some of the ridiculous absurdities of American Whiggism.

I am utterly at a loss what ideas to annex to the phrases "dependence on Great Britain"; "subordination to the Parliament"; "submission to the supreme legislative power"— unless they mean some degree of subjection to the British Parliament, some acknowledgment of its right to make laws to bind the colonies.

Give me leave, sir, to transcribe for your perusal an extract from a petition to the House of Commons, sent by the General Congress, who met at New York the 19th of October, 1765. Whether this Congress was equal in wisdom, dignity, and authority to that lately assembled at Philadelphia, you can determine for yourself. However that be, they express themselves thus:

It is from and under the English constitution we derive

all our civil and religious rights and liberties; we glory in being subjects of the best of kings and having been born under the most perfect form of government. We esteem our connections with, and dependence on, Great Britain as one of our greatest blessings; and apprehend the latter will appear to be sufficiently secure when it is considered that the inhabitants in the colonies have the most unbounded affection for His Majesty's person, family, and government; and that their subordination to the Parliament is universally acknowledged.

A still more respectable body, viz., the General Assembly of New York, in the preamble to their resolutions of the 18th of December 1765, declare:

That they think it their indispensable duty to make a declaration of their faith and allegiance to His Majesty, King George III, and their submission to the supreme legislative power; and at the same time to show that the rights claimed by them are in no manner inconsistent with either.

You have utterly failed in proving that "the clear voice of natural justice" and "the fundamental principles of the English constitution" set us free from the subordination here acknowledged. . . .

Let it be considered that, in every government, legislation and taxation, or the right of raising a revenue, must be conjoined. If you divide them, you weaken and finally destroy the government; for no government can long subsist without power to raise the supplies necessary for its defense and administration.

It has been proved that the supreme authority of the British Empire extends over all the dominions that compose the Empire. The power, or right, of the British Parliament to raise such a revenue as is necessary for the defense and support of the British government in all parts of the British dominions is therefore incontestable. For, if no government can subsist without a power to raise the revenues necessary for its support, then, in fact, no government can extend any further than its power of raising such a revenue extends. If, therefore, the British Parliament has no power to raise a revenue in the colonies, it has no government over the colonies; *i.e.*, no government that can support itself. The burden of supporting its government over the colonies must lie upon the other parts of the Empire.

But this is unreasonable. Government implies not only a power of making and enforcing laws but defense and protection. Now protection implies tribute. Those that share in the protection of any government are in reason and duty bound to maintain and support the government that protects them; otherwise they destroy their own protection; or else they throw an unjust burden on their fellow subjects, which they ought to bear in common with them. While, therefore, the colonies are under the British government and share in its protection, the British government has a right to raise, and they are in reason and duty bound to pay, a reasonable and proportionable part of the expense of its administration.

The authority of the British Parliament, that is, of the supreme sovereign authority of the British Empire, over the colonies, and its right to raise a proportional part of its revenue for the support of its government in the colonies being established, it is to be considered what is the most reasonable and equitable method of doing it. . . .

When it is considered that Great Britain is a maritime power; that the present flourishing state of her trade and of the trade of her colonies depends in a great measure upon the protection which they receive from her Navy; that her own security depends upon her Navy; and that it is principally a naval protection that we receive from her, there will appear a peculiar propriety in laying the chief burden of supporting her Navy upon her commerce, and in requesting us to bear a part of the expense, proportional to our ability, and to that protection and security which we receive from it.

There are but two objections that can reasonably be made to what has been said upon this subject. The first is that, if the British Parliament has a right to make laws to bind the whole Empire, our assemblies become useless. But a little consideration will remove this difficulty.

Our assemblies, from the very nature of things, can have but a legated, subordinate, and local authority of legislation. Their power of making laws in conjunction with the other branches of the legislature cannot extend beyond the limits of the province to which they belong. Their authority must be subordinate to the supreme sovereign authority of the nation, or there is *imperium in imperio*—two sovereign authorities in the same state—which is a contradiction. Everything that relates to the internal policy and government of the province which they represent comes properly before them, whether they be matters of law or revenue. But all laws relative to the Empire in general, or to all the colonies conjunctively, or which regulate the trade of any particular colony, in order to make it compatible with the general good of the whole Empire, must be left to the Parliament. There is no other authority which has a right to make such regulations or weight sufficient to carry them into execution.

Our assemblies are also the true, proper, legal guardians of our rights, privileges, and liberties. . . .

They have always discharged this duty with fidelity, prudence, and firmness; and with such success as ought to encourage us to rely upon their wisdom and good conduct, to deliver us from our present embarrassed state with our mother country; and from that abject slavery and cruel oppression which the tyranny of the late Congress has brought upon us.

Considered in this light, they are a body of real dignity, and of the utmost importance; and whoever attempts to lessen their influence or disparage their authority ought to be considered as an enemy to the liberties of his country. Had our present contests with Great Britain been left to their management, I would not have said a word. But their authority is contravened and superseded by a power from without the province. . . .

You, sir, affect to consider the gentlemen that went from this province to the Congress as the representatives of the province. You know in your conscience that they were not chosen by a hundredth part of the people. You know also that their appointment was in a way unsupported by any law, usage, or custom of the province. You know also that the people of this province had already delegated their power to the members of their Assembly, and therefore had no right to choose delegates, to contravene the authority of the Assembly by introducing a foreign power of legislation. Yet you consider those delegates in a point of light equal to our legal representatives; for you say that "our representatives in General Assembly cannot take any wiser or better course to settle our differences than our representatives in the Continental Congress have taken." Then I affirm that our representatives ought to go to school for seven years before they are returned to serve again. No wiser or better course? Then they must take just the course that the Congress have taken; for a worse, or more foolish, they cannot take should they try; . . .

The other objection to what has been said upon the legislative authority of the British Parliament is this: that if the Parliament have authority to make laws to bind the whole Empire; to regulate the trade of the whole Empire; and to raise a revenue upon the whole Empire, then we have nothing that we can call our own. By the same authority that they can take a penny, they can take a pound, or all we have got. . . .

The colonies have become so considerable by the increase of their inhabitants and commerce, and by the improvement of their lands, that they seem incapable of being governed in the same lax and precarious manner as formerly. They are arrived to that mature state of manhood which requires a different and more exact policy of ruling than was necessary in their infancy and childhood. They want, and are entitled to, a fixed, determinate constitution of their own—a constitution which shall unite them firmly with Great Britain and with one another, which shall mark out the line of British supremacy and colonial dependence, giving, on the one hand, full force to the supreme authority of the nation over all its dominions, and, on the other, securing effectually the rights, liberty, and property of colonists. This is an event devoutly to be wished by all good men, and which all ought to labor to obtain by all prudent and probable means. Without obtaining this, it is idle talk of obtaining a redress of the grievances complained of. They naturally, they necessarily result from the relation which at present stand in to Great Britain.

You, sir, argue through your whole pamphlet upon an assumed point: viz., that the British government—the King, Lords, and Commons—have laid a regular plan to enslave America; and that they are now deliberately putting it in execution. This point has never been proved, though it has been asserted over and over and over again. If you say that they have declared their right of making laws to bind us in all cases whatsoever, I answer that the declarative act here referred to means no more than to assert the supreme authority of Great Britain over all her dominions. If you say that they have exercised this power in a wanton, oppressive manner, it is a point that I am not enough acquainted with the minutiae of government to determine.

It may be true. The colonies are undoubtedly alarmed on account of their liberties. Artful men have availed themselves of the opportunity and have excited such scenes of contention between the parent state and the colonies as afford none but dreadful prospects. Republicans smile at the confusion that they themselves have in a great measure made and are exerting all their influence, by sedition and rebellion, to shake the British Empire to its very basis, that they may have an opportunity of erecting their beloved commonwealth on its ruins. If greater security to our rights and liberties be necessary than the present form and administration of the government can give us, let us endeavor to obtain it; but let our endeavors be regulated by prudence and probability of success. In this attempt all good men will join, both in England and America. All who love their country and wish the prosperity of the British Empire will be glad to see it accomplished.

Before we set out to obtain this security we should have had prudence enough to settle one point among ourselves. We should have considered what security it was we wanted, what concessions on the part of Great Britain would have been sufficient to have fixed our rights and liberties on a firm and permanent foundation. This was the proper business of our assemblies, and to them we ought to have applied. And why we did not apply to them, no one tolerable reason can be assigned—a business which our Assembly, at least, is equal to, whether we consider their abilities as men or their authority as representatives of the province; and a business which, I doubt not, they would have executed with prudence, firmness, and success. . . .

I will here, sir, venture to deliver my sentiments upon the line that ought to be drawn between the supremacy of Great Britain and the dependency of the colonies. And I shall do it with the more boldness because I know it to be agreeable to the opinions of many of the warmest advocates for America, both in England and in the colonies, in the time of the Stamp Act. I imagine that if all internal taxation be vested in our own legislatures, and the right of regulating trade by duties, bounties, etc., be left in the power of the Parliament, and also the right of enacting all general laws for the good of all the colonies, that we shall have all the security for our rights, liberties, and property which human policy can give us. . . .

If we should succeed in depriving Great Britain of the power of regulating our trade, the colonies will probably be soon at variance with each other. Their commercial interests will interfere; there will be no supreme power to interpose, and discord and animosity must ensue.

And upon the whole, if the Parliament can regulate our trade so as to make it conduce to the general good of the whole Empire as well as to our particular profit; if they can protect us in the secure enjoyment of an extensive and lucrative commerce, and at the same time can raise a part of the revenue necessary to support their naval power, without which our commerce cannot be safe, every reasonable man, I should imagine, would think it best to let them enjoy it in peace without descending to the mean, paltry, narrow, stupid design of the Congress.

2

OBSTACLES TO WINNING THE WAR

CHAPTER PREFACE

Once war began in 1775, the Americans encountered a number of problems. The biggest of these was raising an army. Historically, the colonists had relied on local militias to defend against Indians, slave rebellions, and local insurrections. But despite their heroic performances at Lexington, Concord, and Bunker Hill, the militias were no match for British regulars. Upon assuming command of the Continental army, General George Washington began recruiting and training a professional army.

The second problem was equipping the Continental army with the weapons and ammunition it needed to fight, then feeding, sheltering, and clothing it. Unable to provide most of these basic necessities themselves, the Americans looked to Europe for help. Fortunately, they found willing allies in the French, who supplied the Continental army with much of what it needed to fight.

As the war dragged on, the Americans found themselves sorely taxed to keep an army in the field. Relying on volunteers to fill the Continental army's ranks never proved satisfactory, but Congress and the states were unwilling to implement a draft. Since Congress lacked the power to tax, it had to rely on voluntary donations from the states to pay the troops and provide them with food, shelter, and clothing. By war's end, the army was undermanned, underpaid, underfed, poorly equipped, and suffering from low morale.

Meanwhile, the British had their own problems. The Royal Navy was expected to blockade American ports, but it lacked the ships and shore facilities to execute this mission. More seriously, the rebellious colonies sprawled across an expanse of terrain so huge that British troops, by themselves, could not subdue them for any length of time. The British were thus forced to rely on foreign mercenaries and American loyalists, both of whom were in short supply.

Recruiting Soldiers for the Continental Army

Alexander Graydon

After declaring independence in 1776, the Continental Congress found it necessary to recruit an army to defend and protect that independence. Although revolutionary fervor seemed to run high among the upper class, the working class showed a great deal of reluctance to fight for independence. Recruiting officers for the Continental army was relatively easy, but getting working-class Americans to join the army as privates was a problem that Congress was never able to solve satisfactorily. As a result, the armies commanded by General George Washington and other American field commanders rarely included more than a few thousand regular troops. Fortunately for the Americans, these numbers were usually augmented by local militiamen. These irregular troops fought alongside the Continental "bluecoats" whenever there was fighting in the vicinity of their neighborhoods, and they occasionally served with the Continental army for a few months at a time.

Alexander Graydon was a captain in the Continental army. As an officer, one of his duties was to recruit soldiers for the company he commanded. In this selection, he describes the obstacles facing an army recruiter and sheds light on the type of man most likely to join the Continental army.

As you read, consider the following questions:
1. Where does Graydon look first for prospective recruits? How does he try to "sell" army life to his prospects? How does his approach compare to the methods used by present-day military recruiters?

Alexander Graydon, *Memoirs of a Life, Chiefly Passed in Pennsylvania*. Harrisburg, PA, 1811.

2. According to Graydon, why did he have so much trouble getting prospects from "the lower ranks of the people" to join the army? How do present-day political leaders who wish to take their countries to war overcome this problem?

The object now was to raise my company, and as the streets of the city[1] had been pretty well swept by the preceding and contemporary levies, it was necessary to have recourse to the country. My recruiting party was therefore sent out in various directions; and each of my officers as well as myself, exerted himself in the business. Among the many unpleasant peculiarities of the American service, it was not the least that the drudgery, which in old military establishments belongs to serjeants and corporals, here devolved on the commissioned officers; and that the whole business of recruiting, drilling, &c. required their unremitted personal attention. This was more emphatically the case in recruiting; since the common opinion was, that the men and the officers were never to be separated, and hence, to see the persons who were to command them, and above all, the captain, was deemed of vast importance by those inclining to enlist: for this reason I found it necessary, in common with my brother officers, to put my feelings most cruelly to the rack; and in an excursion I once made to Frankford,[2] they were tried to the utmost. A number of fellows at the tavern, at which my party rendezvoused, indicated a desire to enlist, but although they drank freely of our liquor, they still held off. I soon perceived that the object was to amuse themselves at our expense, and that if there might be one or two among them really disposed to engage, the others would prevent them. One fellow in particular, who had made the greatest shew of taking the bounty, presuming on the weakness of our party, consisting only of a drummer, corporal, my second lieutenant and myself, began to grow

1. Philadelphia   2. a town west of Philadelphia

insolent, and manifested an intention to begin a quarrel, in the issue of which, he no doubt calculated on giving us a drubbing. The disgrace of such a circumsts[a]nce, presented itself to my mind in colors the most dismal, and I resolved, that if a scuffle should be unavoidable, it should, at least, be as serious as the hangers[3] which my lieutenant and myself carried by our sides, could make it. Our endeavor, however, was to guard against a contest; but the moderation we testified, was attributed to fear. At length the arrogance of the principal ruffian, rose to such a height, that he squared himself for battle and advanced towards me in an attitude of defiance. I put him by, with an admonition to be quiet, though with a secret determination, that, if he repeated the insult, to begin the war, whatever might be the consequence. The occasion was soon presented; when taking excellent aim, I struck him with the utmost force between the eyes and sent him staggering to the other end of the room. Then instantly drawing our hangers, and receiving the manful co-operation of the corporal and drummer, we were fortunate enough to put a stop to any further hostilities. It was some time before the fellow I had struck, recovered from the blow, but when he did, he was quite an altered man. He was as submissive as could be wished, begging my pardon for what he had done, and although he would not enlist, he hired himself to me for a few weeks as a fifer, in which capacity he had acted in the militia; and during the time he was in this employ, he bore about the effects of his insolence, in a pair of black eyes. This incident would be little worthy of relating, did it not serve in some degree to correct the error of those who seem to conceive the year 1776 to have been a season of almost universal patriotic enthusiasm. It was far from prevalent in my opinion, among the lower ranks of the people, at least in Pennsylvania. At all times, indeed, licentious, levelling principles are much to the general taste, and were of course popular with us; but the true merits of the contest, were little understood

3. A "hanger" was an eighteenth-century light saber.

or regarded. The opposition to the claims of Britain originated with the better sort: it was truly aristocratic in its
commencement; and as the oppression to be apprehended,
had not been felt, no grounds existed for general enthusiasm. The cause of liberty it is true, was fashionable, and
there were great preparations to fight for it; but a zeal proportioned to the magnitude of the question, was only to be
looked for in the minds of those sagacious politicians, who
inferred effects from causes, and who, as Mr. Burke ex-
presses it, "snuffed[4] the approach of tyranny in every
tainted breeze."

Certain it was, at least, that recruiting went on but heavily. Some officers had been more successful than others, but
none of the companies were complete: mine perhaps contained about half its complement of men, and these had
been obtained by dint of great exertion. In this situation,
captain Lenox of Shee's regiment also, suggested the trying
our luck on the Eastern shore of Maryland, particularly at
Chester, situated on the river of that name. It having been a
place of some trade, it was supposed there might be seamen
or *long shore* men there, out of employ. . . . [While in
Chester they find only one recruit.] [He] would do to stop
a bullet as well as a better man, and as he was a truly
worthless dog, . . . the neighborhood would be much in-
debted to us for taking him away. . . .

Returning by Warwick,[5] we sent forward our solitary recruit, for whom we tossed up; and in winning, I was, in
fact, but a very small gainer, . . . he was never fit for any
thing better than the inglorious post of camp colour man.[6]

After this unsuccessful jaunt I bent my course to the
Four-lane ends, Newtown, and Corryell's ferry;[7] thence
passing into Jersey, I proceeded to the Hickory tavern, to
Pittstown, Baptisttown, Flemmingtown, and other towns,
whose names I do not remember. As captain Stewart (the

4. sniffed 5. a town west of Philadelphia 6. the soldier who raises and lowers
the flags while his unit is in camp 7. small towns in Pennsylvania between
Philadelphia and the New Jersey border

late general Walter Stewart) of our regiment, had recently reapt this field, I was only a gleaner: In the whole of my tour, therefore, I picked up but three or four men: and could most sincerely have said,

> That the recruiting trade, with all its train,
> Of endless care, fatigue, and endless pain,

I could most gladly have renounced.

The French Offer Aid to the Americans

Pierre-Augustin Caron de Beaumarchais

Another huge obstacle facing the Americans was the total lack of war materiel with which to outfit an army. Congress established a committee of secret correspondence, in essence the first U.S. State Department, to obtain the needed items from foreign governments. From the start, the French, bitter enemies of the British, agreed to help. Although at first their aid was given clandestinely, eventually the French supplied the United States with a fleet and an army as well.

Pierre-Augustin Caron de Beaumarchais was a French playwright and an agent of the French government. He was also a great admirer of the American struggle for independence, and in 1776 he convinced his government to aid the American cause. With the financial backing of the French government, he opened a commercial house, Roderigue Hortalez and Company, for the primary purpose of providing Americans with the supplies they needed to prosecute the war. He intended to pay for these items by selling American merchandise on the European market, where it commanded a high price.

As you read, consider the following questions:
1. What does Beaumarchais state as his reasons for helping the Americans? Might he have other reasons for helping them as well?
2. Why does Beaumarchais express an interest in Virginia tobacco, and not any other specific commodity?

Pierre-Augustin Caron de Beaumarchais, *Beaumarchais to the Committee of Secret Correspondence of the Continental Congress*, Paris, August 18, 1776.

To the Committee of Secret Correspondence of the Continental Congress.

Paris, August 18, 1776

The respectful esteem that I bear towards that brave people who so well defend their liberty under your conduct has induced me to form a plan concurring in this great work, by establishing an extensive commercial house, solely for the purpose of serving you in Europe, there to supply you with necessaries of every sort, to furnish you expeditiously and certainly with all articles—clothes, linens, powder, ammunition, muskets, cannon, or even gold for the payment of your troops, and in general every thing that can be useful for the honorable war in which you are engaged. Your deputies, gentlemen, will find in me a sure friend, an asylum in my house, money in my coffers, and every means of facilitating their operations, whether of a public or secret nature. I will, if possible, remove all obstacles that may oppose your wishes from the politics of Europe.

At this very time, and without waiting for any answer from you, I have procured for you about two hundred pieces of brass cannon, four-pounders,[1] which will be sent to you by the nearest way, two hundred thousand pounds of cannon powder, twenty thousand excellent fusils,[2] some brass mortars, bombs,[3] cannon balls, bayonets, platines,[4] clothes, linens, etc., for the clothing of your troops, and lead for musket balls. An officer of the greatest merit for artillery and genius, accompanied by lieutenants, officers, artillerists, cannoniers, etc., whom we think necessary for the service, will go for Philadelphia even before you have received my first despatches. This gentlemen is one of the greatest presents that my attachment can offer you. Your deputy, Mr. Deane,[5] agrees with me in the treatment which

1. Cannon were rated by the size of the ball they fired; for example, a four-pounder fired a cannonball weighing approximately four pounds. 2. light flint-lock muskets 3. cannonballs that exploded on impact, like modern artillery shells 4. replacement locks, or firing mechanisms, for the fusils 5. Silas Deane was the first U.S. ambassador to France.

he thinks suitable to his office; and I have found the power of this deputy sufficient that I should prevail with this officer to depart under the sole engagement of the deputy respecting him, the terms of which I have not the least doubt but Congress will comply with.

The secrecy necessary in some part of the operation which I have undertaken for your service requires also, on your part, a formal resolution that all the vessels and their demands should be constantly directed to our house alone, in order that there may be no idle chattering or time lost—two things that are the ruin of affairs. You will advise me what the vessels contain which you shall send into our ports. I shall choose so much of their loading, in return for what I have sent, as shall be suitable to me when I have not been able beforehand to inform you of the cargoes which I wish. I shall facilitate to you the loading, sale and disposal of the rest.

For instance, five American vessels have just arrived in the port of Bordeaux, laden with salt fish. Though this merchandise, coming from strangers, is prohibited in our ports, yet as soon as your deputy had told me that these vessels were sent to him by you to raise money from the sale for aiding him in his purchases in Europe, I took so much care that I secretly obtained from the Farmers-General[6] an order for landing it without any notice being taken of it. I could even, if the case had so happened, have taken on my own account these cargoes of salted fish, though it is no way useful to me, and charged myself with its sale and disposal, to simplify the operation and lessen the embarrassments of the merchants and of your deputy.

I shall have a correspondent in each of our seaport towns who, on the arrival of your vessels, shall wait on the captains and offer every service in my power. He will receive their letters, bills of lading,[7] and transmit the whole to me. Even things which you may wish to arrive safely in any

6. The Farmers-General collected customs duties on goods imported into France.
7. list of trade goods on board a particular ship at a particular time

country in Europe, after having conferred about them with your deputy, I shall cause to be kept in some secure place. Even the answers shall go with great punctuality through me, and this way will save much anxiety and many delays. I request of you, gentlemen, to send me next spring, if it is possible for you, ten or twelve thousand hogsheads, or more if you can, of tobacco from Virginia of the best quality. . . .

I dare promise to you, gentlemen, that my indefatigable zeal shall never be wanting to clear up difficulties, soften prohibitions, and, in short, facilitate all operations of a commerce which my advantage, much less than yours, has made me undertake with you. What I have just informed you of is only a general sketch, subject to all the augmentations and restrictions which events may point out to us.

One thing can never vary or diminish: it is the avowed and ardent desire I have of serving you to the utmost of my power. You will recollect my signature, that one of your friends in London, some time ago, informed you of my favorable disposition towards you and my attachment to your interest. Look upon my house, then, gentlemen, from henceforward as the chief of all useful operations to you in Europe, and my person as one of the most zealous partisans of your cause.

The Problem of Conquering America

William Pitt

When the American Revolution began in earnest in 1776, it seemed certain that the British army would win a quick victory. But the patriot triumphs at Trenton and Princeton that same year and at Saratoga in 1777 made it increasingly unlikely that the British would be able to win the war.

William Pitt, Earl of Chatham, was a prominent member of the House of Lords during the American Revolution. He was more knowledgeable than most British officials about conditions in America, having organized the successful British war effort during the French and Indian War. During the 1760s and early 1770s, he had sympathized with the American colonial position against increased British interference in colonial matters, although he never favored granting them their independence. In this selection from a 1777 speech before the House of Lords in reply to an address by the king, he argues that "you cannot conquer America" and urges the king and Parliament to reconcile with the patriots. The speech was given before word of General John Burgoyne's defeat at Saratoga had reached London, a defeat that gave greater credence to Pitt's speech.

As you read, consider the following questions:
1. Is Pitt right when he claims that "you cannot conquer America"? Under what conditions, if any, could the British have defeated the Americans?
2. Why did Parliament reject Pitt's amendment to its reply to the king's address? Would the king have accepted the amendment if it had passed?

William Pitt, *Anecdotes of the Life of . . . William Pitt, Earl of Chatham*, edited by John Almon. London: J.S. Jordan, 1793.

3. Given the American victory at Saratoga, which occurred thirty-four days before Pitt's speech, how likely is it that the Americans would have accepted a peace based on Pitt's amendment?

My Lords, this ruinous and ignominious situation, where we cannot act with success, nor suffer with honour, calls upon us to remonstrate in the strongest and loudest language of truth to rescue the ear of Majesty from the delusions which surround it. The desperate state of our arms abroad is in part known: no man thinks more highly of them than I do: I love and honour the English troops: I know their virtues and their valor: I know they can achieve anything except impossibilities: and I know that the conquest of English America is an impossibility. You cannot, I venture to say it, you CANNOT conquer America. Your armies last war[1] effected everything that could be effected; and what was it? It cost a numerous army under the command of a most able general, now a noble Lord [Lord Amherst] in this House, a long and laborious campaign, to expel five thousand Frenchmen from French America. My Lords, you *cannot conquer America*. What is your present situation there? We do not know the worst; but we know that in three campaigns we have done nothing, and suffered much. Besides the sufferings, perhaps *total loss* of the Northern force; the best appointed army that ever took the field, commanded by Sir William Howe, has retired from the American lines; he was obliged to relinquish his attempt, and, with great delay and danger, to adopt a new and distant plan of operations. We shall soon know, and in any event have reason to lament, what may have happened since. As to conquest, therefore, my Lords, I repeat it is impossible. You may swell every expense, and every effort still more extravagantly; pile and accumulate every assistance you can buy or borrow; traffic and barter with every

1. the French and Indian War

little pitiful German Prince that sells and sends his subjects to the shambles of a foreign country; your efforts are for ever vain and impotent—doubly so from this mercenary aid on which you rely; for it irritates, to an incurable resentment, the minds of your enemies—to overrun them with the sordid sons of rapine and of plunder; devoting them and their possessions to the rapacity of hireling cruelty! If I were an American, as I am an Englishman, while a foreign troop was landed in my country, I never would lay down my arms; never! never! never! . . .

The Americans, contending for their rights against the arbitrary exactions, I love and admire; it is the struggle of free and virtuous patriots: but contending for independency and total disconnection from England, as an Englishman, I cannot wish them success: for, in a due constitutional dependency, including the ancient supremacy of this country in regulating their commerce and navigation, consists the mutual happiness and prosperity both of England and America. She derived assistance and protection from us; and we reaped from her the most important advantages:—She was, indeed, the fountain of our wealth, the nerve of our strength, the nursery and basis of our naval power. It is our duty, therefore, my Lords, if we wish to save our country, most seriously to endeavour the recovery of these most beneficial subjects: and in this perilous crisis, perhaps the present moment may be the only one in which we can hope for success: for in their negotiations with France, they have, or think they have, reason to complain: though it be notorious that they have received from that power important supplies and assistance of various kinds, yet it is certain they expected it in a more decisive and immediate degree. America is in ill humour with France, on some points that have not entirely answered her expectations: let us wisely take advantage of every possible moment of reconciliation. Besides, the natural disposition of America herself still leans towards England—to the old habits of connection and mutual interest that united both countries. This *was* the established sentiment of all the Continent; and still, my Lords, in the great and principal part, the sound part of America, this wise and affectionate disposition prevails; and there is a very considerable part of America yet sound—the middle and the southern provinces. Some parts may be factious and blind to their true interests; but if we express a wise and benevolent disposition to communicate with them those immutable rights of nature, and those constitutional liberties, to which they are equally entitled with ourselves, by a conduct so just and humane, we shall confirm the favourable and conciliate the adverse. I say, my Lords, the rights and liberties to which they are equally entitled, with ourselves, but no more. I would participate to them every enjoyment and freedom which the colonizing subjects of a free state can possess, or wish to possess; and I do not see why they should not enjoy every fundamental right in their property, and every original substantial liberty, which Devonshire or Surrey, or the county I live in, or any other county in England, can claim; reserving always, as the sacred right of the mother-country, the due constitutional dependency of the Colonies. The inherent supremacy of the State in regulating and protecting the navigation and commerce of all her subjects, is necessary for the mutual benefit and preservation of every part, to constitute and preserve the prosperous arrangement of the whole Empire.

The sound parts of America, of which I have spoken, must be sensible of these great truths and of their real interests. America is not in that state of desperate and contemptible rebellion, which this country has been deluded to believe. It is not a wild and lawless banditti, who having nothing to lose, might hope to snatch something from public convulsions; many of their leaders and great men have a great stake in this great contest:—the gentleman who conducts their armies, I am told, has an estate of four or five thousand pounds a year; and when I consider these things, I cannot but lament the inconsiderate violence of our penal acts, our declarations of treason and rebellion, with all the fatal effects of attainder and confiscation. . . .

What then, can you do? You cannot conquer, you cannot gain, but you can address, you can lull the fears and anxieties of the moment into an ignorance of the danger that should produce them. But, my Lords, the time demands the language of truth: we must not now apply the flattering unction of servile compliance, or blind complaisance. In a just and necessary war, to maintain the rights or honour of my country, I would strip the shirt from my back to support it. But in such a war as this, unjust in its principles, impracticable in its means, and ruinous in its consequences, I would not contribute a single effort, nor a single shilling. . . .

My Lords, to encourage and confirm that innate [American] inclination to this country, founded on every principle of affection, as well as consideration of interest—to restore that favourable disposition into a permanent and powerful reunion with this country—to revive the mutual strength of the empire; again, to awe the House of Bourbon, instead of meanly truckling, as our present calamities compel us, to every insult of French caprice and Spanish punctilio[2]—to reestablish our commerce—to re-assert our rights and our honour—to confirm our interests, and renew our glories for ever (a consummation most devoutly to be endeavoured! and which, I trust, may yet arise from reconciliation with America)—I have the honour of submitting to you the following amendment, which I move to be inserted after the two first paragraphs of the Address:—

'And that this House does most humbly advise and supplicate his Majesty to be pleased to cause the most speedy and effectual measures to be taken for restoring peace in America; and that no time may be lost in proposing an immediate cessation of hostilities there, in order to the opening a treaty for the final settlement of the tranquillity of these invaluable provinces, by a removal of the unhappy causes of this ruinous civil war; and by a just and adequate

2. The Spanish were allied with the French during the American Revolution, and fought against the British in Europe, Florida, Central America, and the Caribbean.

security against the return of the like calamities in times to come. And this House desire to offer the most dutiful assurances to his Majesty, that they will, in due time, cheerfully co-operate with the magnanimity and tender goodness of his Majesty for the preservation of his people, by such explicit and most solemn declarations and provisions of fundamental and irrevocable laws, as may be judged necessary for the ascertaining and fixing for ever the respective rights of Great Britain and her colonies."[3]

3. The amendment was rejected by a vote of 97 to 24.

Maintaining a British Fleet in America

John Montagu

One thing the British had hoped to be able to do during the war was to blockade American ports, thus keeping in the Continental navy and American privateers while keeping out supplies and other aid from Europe. However, the immense length of the American coastline, the lack of friendly ports in which to obtain supplies and repairs, and the constant demands made on the navy by the Royal Army made such a blockade virtually impossible.

John Montagu, Earl of Sandwich, was first lord of the admiralty, and therefore in charge of the Royal Navy. Frederick Lord North was the British prime minister, and therefore in charge of continuing Parliament's support for the war. In this selection from a letter to North dated December 8, 1777, Montagu recounts the difficulties the Royal Navy had encountered during the first two years of the war. He also relates his fears that France and Spain might soon enter the war as American allies, in which case the English coast might be in danger of being invaded by a Franco-Spanish armada.

As you read, consider the following questions:
1. What was the biggest problem faced by the British fleet in America? Why?
2. How realistic is Montagu's fear that a combined Franco-Spanish fleet might invade or harass the English coast? How might this threat affect Britain's ability or desire to provide its fleet in America with the extra ships and supplies that Montagu thinks it needs?

John Montagu, *Earl of Sandwich to Lord North*, December 8, 1777.

The mode of carrying on the war in America has been such for the last two years that the fleet has not been employed in the purposes in which it can be most useful towards distressing the enemy, and making them feel their inability of holding out against the mother country.

Lord Howe[1] has had this year under his command about 90 ships of all sorts, six of them of the line[2] and ten two-deck ships, that is to say ships of fifty and forty-four guns; and it was natural to suppose that with such a force properly stationed he could have made it very difficult for the Americans to receive their supplies, carry on their trade, and fit out privateers to annoy the trade of Great Britain. The contrary however has been the case because the greatest part of Lord Howe's fleet has been employed in convoying, embarking and disembarking the troops, and attending the operations of the army, which his Lordship in his first letters after his arrival in America mentions as his principal object, to which all others must give place. I do not mean to say that this was wrong, but the consequence of it was that our trade suffered, and that the enemy got the supplies from Europe by which they have been enabled to resist us.

It must not however be imagined that any force will be sufficient entirely to execute the purpose of blocking up all the rebels' ports and putting a total stop to their privateering; for along so extensive a coast, full of harbours and inlets, many ships will in spite of all our efforts get in and out by taking advantage of their knowledge of the coast, of dark and long nights, and events of wind and weather favourable to their purposes. However, we may certainly distress them infinitely more than has hitherto been done, and throw such burdens upon their trade and privateering as to make it difficult to carry on either without consider-

1. Admiral Richard, Lord Howe was the commander in chief of the Royal Navy in America.   2. A ship of the line was an eighteenth-century battleship and was armed with sixty or more guns.

able loss, which, it is to be hoped, together with their want of necessaries from Europe, would soon make them tired of the war.

But in order to be able to employ the naval force in America effectually to this purpose, it is absolutely necessary that the army should secure the possession of several places along the coast which are tenable (independent of a fleet to defend them) against any force the Americans can bring against them. These places must be such as the King's ships can resort to at all times and seasons, and which will give them shelter and refreshments for their men; and it is necessary that one of them at least (exclusive of Halifax[3]) should afford complete and secure conveniences for careening[4] and refitting the ships, without which both the ships and men will soon become unfit for cruising, which is to be feared is already the case of many of Lord Howe's squadron.

Such ports are absolutely necessary, and without them no such naval war as is now recommended can be maintained so as to answer the purposes expected; for it must be remembered that cruisers can keep the sea only for a limited time, and that they must have friendly ports to repair to, to wood and water, and to supply their want of stores, and repair their defects, as also for the preservation of the health of their people. This was the idea of the Admiralty from the beginning of the war, and Lord Howe was accordingly by his instructions directed to consider and propose to us what ports were in his opinion properest for these purposes; but he has as yet made no return thereupon.

To supply what has been omitted in this particular, I would propose that a commissioner of the navy with proper assistants should go over in the first ships, with power to make such naval establishment and in such place as upon consulting with Lord Howe shall be thought most advisable. New York, Rhode Island, or Philadelphia, would in all probability effectually answer these purposes;

3. The Royal Navy maintained a state-of-the-art shipyard in Halifax, Nova Scotia.
4. tipping a ship on its side so its bottom can be repaired

but it is impossible to decide the point at this distance, and therefore I would leave it to be settled on the spot and with Lord Howe's advice, who from the experience he has had and his local knowledge will be, it is to be presumed, a perfect master of the subject.

The Navy Board should be directed to send out what materials and artificers they may think proper for the beginning such establishment; but as it will take some time before this business can be completed, particular attention should be had, and immediate orders given, to provide for the security of Halifax, which since the late fatal event[5] is in my opinion in imminent danger of an attack from New England early in the spring. If that important place should fall into the hands of the enemy, it would be a blow not easy to be recovered, as it is the only port in the whole continent of America where ships can be cleaned and refitted at this time, and is the seat of a commissioner of the navy with an established naval yard and proper artificers and materials for carrying on the business. It is to be always remembered that the fleet alone cannot defend the place, and that there must be a reinforcement of troops and additional works, if the present are not sufficient to repel every attempt of an enemy. While the American forces were employed at a distance, and the people of New England were expecting an attack at home, a small garrison was sufficient, but that is no longer the case, and as the rebels have no better means of employing their northern army than in attacking Canada or Halifax, and probably both, it seems to be our duty to attend to the security of these very important posts.

And for the better carrying on the naval service in that very extensive continent, it seems advisable that the command should be divided into two parts at least, viz the northern and southern; the first to include all Nova Scotia and Canada, the other from the Bay of Boston inclusive to Georgia. . . .

5. Montagu refers to the defeat and capture of General John Burgoyne's army at Saratoga, New York.

It is much to be wished that a separate command was also fixed in the southern colonies; and perhaps Port Royal in South Carolina would be a very proper place for the headquarters of that squadron. But I fear that at present this arrangement cannot be executed, for unless we are masters of the shore by means of our army, or by the good-will of the inhabitants, none of the purposes wanted for the fitting and refreshing our ships can be obtained; and I can see nothing more to be done with regard to that district as yet than to leave it as it now is, giving directions to Lord Howe to employ as many cruisers to the southward as he can possibly spare, and to relieve them from time to time from his central post. . . .

Lord Howe should be told that his principal object now should be to block up the American ports. . . . He should keep as many cruisers at sea in small squadrons as his force will enable him to do; and it should be pointed out to him to be particularly attentive to the sending frequent intelligence to England of any armed vessels fitting out in America, for want of which 18 rebel privateers of whose existence we had no intelligence from his Lordship sailed at once from Boston and Salem and came upon us unprepared in different parts, having appeared first on the Banks of Newfoundland where they took the *Fox* and did considerable damage to the fishery, while others attacked the homeward-bound West India convoy, and some had the audaciousness to insult our own coast and the trade in the British Channel.

It seems to me to be within the scope of the present subject to say a word or two on the state of our naval force at home . . . and to consider whether it is adequate to the services that may be expected from it. We have 42 ships of the line in commission at home, which may fairly be considered as ready for service. I fear that France and Spain united have at least an equal number in Europe in commission, and I believe they have many more ready to receive men. I observe that France has only sent one ship of the line out of Europe, therefore her whole naval force may be said to be at home. Spain has no less than 42 ships of the line in

French and British fleets clash off Cape Henry in 1781. The British had hoped to keep supplies from reaching America by blockading its ports.

commission, many of which are in foreign parts; and they certainly already have or can collect a formidable fleet at Havana [Cuba] without detaching from Europe. . . .

We are vulnerable by a fleet at Jamaica, the Leeward Islands, and in North America, even without the aid of land forces; and with their aid, in the East Indies, and (if the Governor of Gibraltar's late account is true that he cannot defend the place without double his present garrison) in the Mediterranean also.

As soon as France determines to make war a squadron will be sent to attack us in one of these parts. We shall not know where the storm will fall, therefore the only measure of safety will be to have a respectable force in every part. . . . Will our 42 ships supply the necessary detachments to answer this purpose, and to leave us superior at home to anything the House of Bourbon can bring against us in Europe after their detachment is made? Certainly not. Therefore, unless we are sure that France has no hostile intentions, is it prudent for us to remain a moment longer in our present state?

It will take a twelvemonth to get 25 more ships of the line ready for sea; 7 of the 25 (including *Victory*) are now ready to receive men, and if they were commissioned would be ready for sea early in the spring; and 7 others would be immediately taken in hand, and ready to be commissioned in about two months. If we are in imminent danger of a foreign war (which in my opinion is the case), a day ought not to be lost. What shall we have to answer for if we are taken unprepared, and reduced to the necessity of either leaving our distant possessions undefended or seeing France and Spain in the Channel with a superior fleet?

In short, if we are certain that France and Spain will not take advantage of our distresses, our force at home is more than sufficient, and the public ought not to be burdened with that enormous expense; but on the other side, if from their falsehood and repeated breaches of their most solemn promises relative to succours sent to America, . . . we may conclude that they are at the bottom our inveterate enemies, and are only waiting for the favourable moment to strike the blow, I do think we risk the whole with regard to the safety of our country if we are any way remiss in using every precaution and exertion for our defence that our present circumstances require.

I would therefore humbly advise that the 7 ships now ready to receive men, or at least 6 of them, should be commissioned, and that orders should be given for getting an equal number ready to receive men. Before it comes to their turn to be commissioned, events will show whether it is necessary to proceed farther.

Keeping an American Army in the Field

George Washington

Throughout the duration of the war, the Continental army relied on volunteers to fill its ranks. Most volunteers enlisted for only three months, so as soon as they were trained and equipped it was time for them to go home. One result was much wasted effort by officers and drill sergeants, who spent most of their time training new soldiers. Another result was an army full of green recruits who, despite their training, were usually unable to exploit favorable developments on the battlefield.

George Washington was the commander-in-chief of the Continental army. In this selection from a letter he sent to the governors of the various states, he outlines the problems he faced by having to rely on short-term volunteers and militiamen. As a solution to this problem, he calls for the establishment of a permanent army.

As you read, consider the following questions:
1. Washington seems to blame short enlistments for all of the problems he faced in battle. Does his assessment seem reasonable? If so, why? If not, why not?
2. By 1780, when this piece was written, Americans were suffering from war weariness. How enthusiastically do you think they might have embraced the establishment of a permanent army, probably via a national draft or some similar means, like the one Washington proposes? What might have been the result of the war had a draft been implemented?

George Washington, *Circular to the State Governors*, October 18, 1780.

Head Quarters, near Passaic Falls,[1] October 18, 1780. Sir: In obedience to the orders of Congress, I have the honor to transmit you the present state of the troops of your line, by which you will perceive how few Men you will have left after the 1st of Jany. next.[2] When I inform you also that the Regiments of the other Lines will be in general as much reduced as yours, you will be able to judge how exceedingly weak the Army will be at that period, and how essential it is the states should make the most vigorous exertions to replace the discharged Men as early as possible.

Congress are now preparing a plan for a new establishment of their Army which when finished they will transmit to the several States with requisitions for their respective quotas. I have no doubt it will be a primary object with them to have the Levies for the War, and this appears to me a point so interesting to our Independence that I cannot forbear entering into the motives which ought to determine the States without hesitation or alternative to take their measures decisively for that object.

I am religiously persuaded that the duration of the War and the greatest part of the misfortunes and perplexities we have hitherto experienced, are chiefly to be attributed to the System of temporary enlistments. Had we in the commencement raised an Army for the War, such as was within the reach of the Abilities of these States to raise and maintain we should not have suffered those military Checks which have so frequently shaken our cause, nor should we have incurred such enormous expenditures as have destroyed our paper Currency and with it all public credit. A moderate compact force on a permanent establishment capable of acquiring the discipline essential to military operations would have been able to make head against the enemy without comparison better than the throngs of Militia which at certain periods have been, not in the field, but in their way to and from the Field; for from that want of perseverance

1. New Jersey   3. January 1, 1781, when a number of enlistments expired

which characterises all Militia, and of that coercion which cannot be exercised upon them, it has always been found impracticable to detain the greatest part of them in service even for the term, for which they have been called out, and this has been commonly so short, that we have had a great proportion of the time two sets of Men to feed and pay, one coming to the Army and the other going from it. From this circumstance and from the extraordinary waste and consumption of provisions, stores, Camp equipage, Arms, Cloaths and every other Article incident to irregular troops, it is easy to conceive what an immense increase of public expence has been produced from the source of which I am speaking. I might add the diminution of our Agriculture by calling off at critical Seasons the labourers employed in it, as has happened in instances without number.

In the enumeration of Articles wasted, I mention Cloathes. It may be objected that the terms of engagements of the Levies do not include this, but if we want service from the Men particularly in the cold Season we are obliged to supply them notwithstanding, and they leave us before the Cloaths are half worn out.

But there are evils still more striking that have befallen us. The intervals between the dismission of one Army and the collection of another have more than once threatened us with ruin, which humanly speaking nothing but the supineness or folly of the enemy could have saved us from. How did our cause totter at the close of 76, when with a little more than two thousand Men we were driven before the enemy thro' Jersey and obliged to take post on the other side of the Delaware to make a shew of covering Philadelphia while in reallity nothing was more easy to them with a little enterprise, and industry than to make their passage good to that City and dissipate the remaining force which still kept alive our expiring opposition! What hindered them from dispersing our little Army and giving a fatal Blow to our affairs during all the subsequent winter, instead of remaining in a state of torpid inactivity and permitting us to hover about their Quarters when we had scarcely troops sufficient to mount the ordinary Guard? After having lost two Battles and Philadelphia in the following Campaign for want of those numbers and that degree of discipline which we might have acquired by a permanent force in the first instance, in what a cruel and perilous situation did we again find ourselves in the Winter of 77 at Valley Forge, within a days march of the enemy, with a little more than a third of their strength, unable to defend our position, or retreat from it, for want of the means of transportation? What but the fluctuation of our Army enabled the enemy to detach so boldly to the southward in 78 and 79 to take possession of the two States Georgia and South Carolina, while we were obliged here to be idle Spectators of their weakness; set at defiance by a Garrison of six thousand regular troops, accessible every where by a Bridge which nature had formed, but of which we were unable to take advantage from still greater weakness, apprehensive even for our own safety? How did the same Garrison insult the main Army of these States the ensuing Spring and threaten the destruction of all our Baggage and Stores, saved by a good countenance more than by an ability to defend them? And what will be our situation this winter, our Army by the 1st. of January diminished to a little more than a sufficient Garrison for West point, the enemy at liberty to range the Country wherever they please, and, leaving a handful of Men at N York, to undertake Expeditions for the reduction of other States, which for want of adequate means of defense will it is much to be dreaded add to the number of their conquests and to the examples of our want of energy and wisdom?

. . . The immediate prospect of being left without Troops

George Washington

might be enumerated in the catalogue of evils that have sprang from this fruitful source. We not only incur these dangers and suffer these losses for want of a constant force equal to our exigencies, but while we labor under this impediment it is impossible there can be any order or economy or system in our finances. If we meet with any severe blow the great exertions which the moment requires to stop the progress of the misfortune oblige us to depart from general principles to run into any expence or to adopt any expedient however injurious on a larger scale to procure the force and means which the present emergency demands. Every thing is thrown into confusion and the measures taken to remedy immediate evils perpetuate others. The same is the case if particular conjunctions invite us to offensive operations; we find ourselves unprepared without troops, without Magazines, and with little time to provide them. We are obliged to force our resources by the most burthensome methods to answer the end, and after all it is but half answered: the design is announced by the occasional effort, and the enemy have it in their power to counteract and elude the blow. The prices of every thing, Men provisions &ca. are raised to a height to which the Revenues of no Government, much less ours, would suffice. It is impossible the people can endure the excessive burthen of bounties for annual drafts and substitutes increasing at every new experiment: whatever it might cost them once for all to procure Men for the War would be a cheap bargain.

I am convinced our System of temporary inlistments has prolonged the War and encouraged the enemy to persevere. Baffled while we had an Army in the field, they have been constantly looking forward to the period of its reduction, as the period to our opposition, and the season of their successes. They have flattered themselves with more than the event has justified; for they believed when one Army expired, we should not be able to raise another: undeceived however in this expectation by experience, they still remained convinced, and to me evidently on good grounds, that we must ultimately sink under a system which increases our expense beyond calculation, enfeebles all our measures, affords the most inviting opportunities to the enemy, and wearies and disgusts the people. This has doubtless had great influence in preventing their coming to terms and will continue to operate in the same way. The debates on the ministerial side have frequently manifested the operation of this motive, and it must in the nature of things have had great weight.

The interpositions of Neutral powers may lead to a negociation this winter: Nothing will tend so much to make the Court of London reasonable as the prospect of a permanent Army in this Country, and a spirit of exertion to support it.

Tis time we should get rid of an error which the experience of all mankind has exploded, and which our own experience has dearly taught us to reject; the carrying on a War with Militia, or, (which is nearly the same thing) temporary levies against a regular, permanent and disciplined force. The Idea is chimerical, and that we have so long persisted in it is a reflection on the judgment of a Nation so enlightened as we are, as well as a strong proof of the empire of prejudice over reason. If we continue in the infatuation, we shall deserve to lose the object we are contending for.

America has been almost amused out of her liberties. We have frequently heard the behavior of the Militia extolled upon one and another occasion by Men who judge only from the surface, by Men who had particular views in misrepresenting, by visionary Men whose credulity easily swallowed every vague story in support of a favorite Hypothesis. I solemnly declare I never was witness to a single instance that can countenance an opinion of Militia or raw troops being fit for the real business of fighting. I have found them useful as light parties to skirmish the Woods, but incapable of making or sustaining a serious attack. This firmness is only acquired by habit of discipline and service. I mean not to detract from the merit of the Militia; their zeal and spirit upon a variety of occasions have intitled them to the highest applause; but it is of the greatest importance we should learn to estimate them rightly. We may expect everything from ours that Militia is capable of, but we must not expect from any, service for which Regulars alone are fit. The late Battle of Campden[3] is a melancholy comment upon this doctrine. The Militia fled at the first fire, and left the Continental troops surrounded on every side and overpowered by numbers to combat for safety instead of Victory. The enemy themselves have witnessed to their Valor.

An ill effect of short enlistments which I have not yet taken notice of, is that the constant fluctuation of their Men is one of the sources of disgust to the Officers. Just when by great trouble fatigue and vexation (with which the training of Recruits is attended) they have brought their Men to some kind of order, they have the mortification to see them go home, and to know that the drudgery is to recommence the next Campaign. In Regiments so constituted, an Officer has neither satisfaction nor credit in his command.

Every motive which can arise from a consideration of our circumstances, either in a domestic or foreign point of view calls upon us to abandon temporary expedients and substitute something durable, systematic and substantial. . . .

The Army is not only dwindling into nothing, but the discontents of the Officers as well as the Men have matured to a degree that threatens but too general a renunciation of the service, at the end of the Campaign. Since January last we have had registered at Head Quarters more than one hundred and sixty resignations, besides a number of others that were never regularly reported. I speak of the Army in this Quarter. We have frequently in the course of the Campaign experienced an extremity of want. Our Officers are in general indecently defective in Cloathing. Our Men are almost naked, totally unprepared for the inclemency of the approaching season. We have no magazines for the Winter; the mode of procuring our supplies is precarious, and all the reports of the Officers employed in collecting them are gloomy.

3. Two months earlier, an American army under General Horatio Gates had been completely routed at Camden, South Carolina.

These circumstances conspire to show the necessity of immediately adopting a plan that will give more energy to Government, more vigor and more satisfaction to the Army. Without it we have every thing to fear. I am persuaded of the sufficiency of our resources if properly directed.

Should the requisitions of Congress by any accident not arrive before the Legislature is about to rise, I beg to recommend that a plan be devised, which is likely to be effectual, for raising the Men that will be required for the War, leaving it to the Executive to apply it to the Quota which Congress will fix. I flatter myself however the requisition will arrive in time.

The present Crisis of our Affairs appears to me so serious as to call upon me as a good Citizen to offer my sentiments freely for the safety of the Republic. I hope the motive will excuse the liberty I have taken.

Financing the American War Effort

Robert Morris

Next to recruiting troops, the biggest obstacle to prosecuting the American war effort was paying the army's salaries and providing it with supplies. The Continental Congress did not have the power to tax, so it tried to fund the war effort by asking the states to provide money and materiel in relation to each state's supposed wealth and in accordance to how much Congress had spent for that state's defense. Meanwhile, the states were struggling to pay and supply their own militias and navies, and most never satisfied the requests made on them by Congress. As a result, Congress was forced to pay for the war by issuing almost $250 million in paper money. Known as Continental dollars, by 1780 this currency was virtually worthless, thus giving rise to the phrase "not worth a continental."

In 1781 Congress appointed Robert Morris, a Philadelphia merchant and financier, as superintendent of finance. He immediately set about putting Congress's finances on a sound footing. In this selection, a blanket letter to the governors of all thirteen states, he asks that the states settle their accounts with Congress as soon as possible.

As you read, consider the following questions:
1. How does Morris intend to get the states to pay their accounts in full? Does this method sound like it could work? Did it work?
2. What changes would you make to Congress's duties and powers so that the financial difficulties experienced by Morris might be avoided during future wars?

Robert Morris, *Morris to the Governors of the States*, Philadelphia, July 25, 1781.

Sir: I had the honor to write to you on the—instant,[1] enclosing a certified copy of the account of your State as it stands in the treasury books of the United States. I now pray leave to recall your attention to it.

It gives me very great pain to learn that there is a pernicious idea prevalent among some of the States that their accounts are not to be adjusted with the continent.[2] Such an idea can not fail to spread listless languor over all our operations. To suppose this expensive war can be carried on without joint and strenuous efforts is beneath the wisdom of those who are called to the high offices of legislation. Those who inculcate maxims which tend to relax these efforts most certainly injure the common cause, whatever may be the motives which inspire their conduct. If once an opinion is admitted that those States who do the least and charge most will derive the greatest benefit and endure the smallest evils, your excellency must perceive that shameless inactivity must take the place of that noble emulation which ought to pervade and animate the whole Union. It is my particular duty, while I remind my fellow-citizens of the tasks which it is incumbent on them to perform, to remove, if I can, every impediment which lies in the way, or which may have been raised by disaffection, self-interest, or mistake. I take, therefore, this early opportunity to assure you that all the accounts of the several States with the United States shall be speedily liquidated if I can possibly effect it, and my efforts for that purpose shall be unceasing. I make this assurance in the most solemn manner, and I entreat that the consequences of a contrary assertion may be most seriously weighed and considered before it is made or believed.

These accounts . . . must be adjusted as soon as proper officers can be found and appointed for the purpose and proper principles established, so as that they may be liquidated in an equitable manner. I say, sir, in an equitable manner; for I am determined that justice shall be the rule of my

1. earlier this month 2. paid in full

conduct as far as the measure of abilities which the Almighty has been pleased to bestow shall enable me to distinguish between right and wrong. I shall never permit a doubt that the States will do what is right; neither will I ever believe that any one of them can expect to derive advantage from doing what is wrong. It is by being just to individuals, to each other, to the Union, to all; by generous grants of solid revenue, and by adopting energetic methods to collect that revenue; and not by complainings, vauntings, or recriminations, that these States must expect to establish their independence and rise into power, consequence, and grandeur. I speak to your excellency with freedom, because it is my duty so to speak, and because I am convinced that the language of plain sincerity is the only proper language to the first magistrate of a free community.

The accounts . . . admit of an immediate settlement. The several States have all the necessary materials. One side of this account consists of demands made by resolutions of Congress long since forwarded; the other must consist of the compliances with those demands. This latter part I am not in a capacity to state, and for that reason I am to request the earliest information which the nature of things will permit of the moneys, supplies, transportation, &c., which have been paid, advanced, or furnished by your State, in order that I may know what remains due. The sooner full information can be obtained the sooner shall we know what to rely on, and how to do equal justice to those who have contributed and those who have not; to those who have contributed at one period and those who have contributed at another.

I enclose an account of the specific supplies demanded of your State, as extracted from the journals of Congress, but without any mention of what has been done in consequence of those resolutions; because, as I have already observed, your excellency will be able to discover the balance much better than I can.

I am further to entreat, sir, that I may be favored with copies of the several acts passed in your State . . . for the collection of taxes and the furnishing supplies or other aids to the United States, the manner in which such acts have been executed, the times which may have been necessary for them to operate, and the consequences of their operation. I must also pray to be informed of so much of the internal police of your State as relates to the laying, assessing, levying, and collecting taxes. I beg leave to assure your excellency that I am not prompted either by an idle curiosity or by any wish to discover what prudence would dictate to conceal. It is necessary that I should be informed of these things, and I take the plain, open, candid method of acquiring information. To palliate or conceal any evils or disorders in our situation can answer no good purpose; they must be known before they can be cured. We must also know what resources can be brought forth, that we may proportion our efforts to our means and our demands to both. It is necessary that we should be in condition to prosecute the war with ease before we can expect to lay down our arms with security, before we can treat of peace honorably, and before we can conclude it with advantage. I feel myself fettered at every moment and embarrassed in every operation from my ignorance of our actual state and of what is reasonably to be asked or expected. Yet when I consider our real wealth and numbers, and when I compare them with those of other countries, I feel a thorough conviction that we may do much more than we have yet done, and with more ease to ourselves than we have yet felt, provided we adopt the proper modes of revenue and expenditure.

Your excellency's good sense will anticipate my observations on the necessity of being informed what moneys are in your treasury and what sums you expect to have there, as also the times by which they must probably be brought in. In addition to this, I must pray you to communicate the several appropriations.

A misfortune peculiar to America requires that I entreat your excellency to undertake one more task, which, perhaps, is far from being the least difficult. It is, sir, that you will write me very fully as to the amount of the several paper currencies now circulating in your State, the probable increase or decrease of each, and the respective rates of depreciation.

Having now stated the several communications which are most indispensable, let me entreat of your excellency's goodness that they may be made as speedily as possible, to the end that I may be early prepared with those propositions which, from a view of all circumstances, may be most likely to extricate us from our present difficulties. I am also to entreat that you will inform me when your legislature is to meet. My reason for making this request is, that any proposals to be made to them may arrive in season for their attentive deliberation.

I know that I give you much trouble, but I also know that it will be pleasing to you, because the time and labor will be expended in the service of your country. If, sir, my feeble but honest efforts should open to us the prospect of American glory, if we should be enabled to look forward to a period when, supported by solid revenue and resources, this war should have no other duration or extent than the wisdom of Congress might allow, and when its object should be the honor and not the independence of our country; if with these fair views the States should be roused, excited, animated, in the pursuit and unitedly determining to be in that happy situation find themselves placed there by the very determination—if, sir, these things should happen, and what is more if they should happen soon, the reflection that your industry has principally contributed to effect them would be the rich reward of your toils, and give to your best feelings their amplest gratification.

CHAPTER

3

THE WAR

CHAPTER PREFACE

The war affected everyone in America, usually for the worse. Obviously, the most profound impact was felt by soldiers. Congress provided the rank and file of the Continental army with just enough food, shelter, and clothing to make life bearable. At times, such as during the harsh winter of 1777–1778 at Valley Forge, even the minimum requirements to sustain life were scarce. As gentlemen, officers usually led a better lifestyle. While the privates shivered in their lean-tos at Valley Forge, many officers found accommodations in the homes of local farmers. Even so, officers, like the men who served under them, were usually poorly supplied and paid.

Next to soldiers, loyalists were most affected by the war. Everyone suspected of being pro-British was harassed by the local militias until they declared their devotion to the American cause. Those who persisted in their loyalty to the king were run out of town, imprisoned, or even killed.

Civilians suffered from the uncertainty of war. Whenever the armies were on the march, local people feared they would be robbed, raped, left homeless, or murdered by undisciplined troops. Toward the end of the war, when the British were desperate to bring things to an end, redcoats often targeted the homes and property of patriot civilians for plundering and destruction.

While the men fought, their women carried on at home. Usually this meant tending the family farm or business with the help of whatever friends, relatives, or neighbors they could muster. In many cases, women went to war with their men. Neither army possessed a commissary or medical corps, so women often accompanied the armies to serve as cooks, nurses, and laundresses for their male relatives. In rare instances, women such as Molly Pitcher and Deborah Sampson even took up arms and fought alongside their men.

For some, the war was an exciting experience. It gave teenage girls the opportunity to meet and mingle with dashing young officers from other states. It also gave small boys the opportunity to dream dreams of military glory, innocent as they were of the death and destruction that war invariably brings.

A Connecticut Private Describes a Soldier's Existence

Joseph Plumb Martin

The lot of a soldier in the Continental army was pretty dismal. Throughout the war, the army was underfed, poorly clothed, poorly shod, and poorly provisioned with such essentials as tents, blankets, and medical supplies. To make matters worse, the army was rarely paid on time, and many soldiers never received what was owed them. By 1783, things had become so bad that hundreds of Pennsylvania troops, having just been discharged from the army without any provisions whatsoever concerning their back pay, marched on the state house in Philadelphia and briefly held the Continental Congress, which was meeting inside, as hostages.

Joseph Plumb Martin was a private in the Continental army's Connecticut Line. He kept a diary during the war, and shortly afterward he wrote a narrative about his experiences in the army. In this excerpt, he describes the hardships faced by common soldiers in the days leading up to the army going into winter quarters at and around Valley Forge in late 1777.

As you read, consider the following questions:
1. Why were Martin and his fellow soldiers so poorly provisioned?
2. Why did Martin and his fellow soldiers continue to serve under such detestable conditions?

Joseph Plumb Martin, *A Narrative of Some of the Adventures, Dangers, and Sufferings of a Revolutionary Soldier, Interspersed with Anecdotes That Occurred Within His Own Observation.* Hallowell, ME, 1830.

We now prepared to leave Red Bank.[1] I was ordered on a baggage guard; it was not disagreeable to me as I had a chance to ride in a wagon a considerable part of the night. We went in advance of the troops, which made it much easier getting along. We had been encouraged during the whole siege with the promise of relief. "Stand it out a little longer and we shall be relieved," had been the constant cry. The second day of our march we met two regiments advancing to relieve us. When asked where they were going, they said to relieve the garrison in the fort. We informed them that the British had done that already. . . .

We arrived early in the morning at a pretty village called Milltown or Mount Holly. Here we waited for the troops to come up. I was as near starved with hunger as ever I wish to be. I strolled into a large yard where was several sawmills and a gristmill. I went into the latter, thinking it probable that the dust made there was more palatable than that made in the former, but I found nothing there to satisfy my hunger. But there was a barrel standing behind the door with some salt in it. Salt was as valuable as gold with the soldiers. I filled my pocket with it and went out. In the yard and about it was a plenty of geese, turkeys, ducks, and barn-door fowls. I obtained a piece of an ear of Indian corn, and seating myself on a pile of boards, began throwing the corn to the fowls, which soon drew a fine battalion of them about me. I might have taken as many as I pleased, but I took up one only, wrung off its head, dressed and washed it in the stream, seasoned it with some of my salt, and stalked into the first house that fell in my way, invited myself into the kitchen, took down the gridiron and put my fowl to cooking upon the coals. The women of the house were all the time going and coming to and from the room. They looked at me but said nothing. "They asked me no questions and I told them no lies." When my game was sufficiently broiled, I took it by the *hind* leg and made my exit

1. Martin's unit was abandoning Fort Mercer in Red Bank, New Jersey, to the British.

from the house with as little ceremony as I had made my entrance. When I got into the street I devoured it after a *very* short grace and felt as refreshed as the old Indian did when he had eaten his crow roasted in the ashes with the feathers and entrails.

We marched from hence and crossed the Delaware again between Burlington and Bristol. Here we procured a day's ration of southern salt pork (three fourths of a pound) and a pound of sea bread. We marched a little distance and stopped "to refresh ourselves." We kindled some fires in the road, and some broiled their meat; as for myself, I ate mine raw. We quickly started on and marched till evening, when we went into a wood for the night. We did not pitch our tents, and about midnight it began to rain very hard, which soon put out all our fires and we had to lie "and weather it out." The troops marched again before day. I had sadly sprained my ankle the day before and it was much swelled. My lieutenant told me to stay where I was till day and then come on. . . . I had finished my pork and bread for supper, consequently had nothing for this day. I hobbled on as well as I could. The rain and traveling of the troops and baggage had converted the road into perfect mortar and it was extremely difficult for me to make headway. I worried on, however, till sometime in the afternoon, when I went into a house where I procured a piece of a buckwheat slapjack.[2] With this little refreshment I proceeded on and just before night overtook the troops. We continued our march until sometime after dark, when we arrived in the vicinity of the main army. We again turned into a wood for the night. The leaves and ground were as wet as water could make them. It was then foggy and the water dropping from the trees like a shower. We endeavored to get fire by flashing powder on the leaves, but this and every other expedient that we could employ failing, we were forced by our old master, Necessity, to lay down and sleep if we could, with three others of our constant com-

2. a type of pancake

panions, Fatigue, Hunger, and Cold.

Next morning we joined the grand army near Philadelphia, and the heavy baggage being sent back to the rear of the army, we were obliged to put us up huts by laying up poles and covering them with leaves, a capital shelter from winter storms. Here we continued to fast; indeed we kept a continual Lent as faithfully as ever any of the most rigorous of the Roman Catholics did. But there was this exception, we had no fish or eggs or any other substitute for our commons. Ours was a real fast and, depend upon it, we were sufficiently mortified.

About this time the whole British army left the city, came out, and encamped, or rather lay, on Chestnut Hill in our immediate neighborhood. We hourly expected an attack from them; we had a commanding position and were very sensible of it. We were kept constantly on the alert, and wished nothing more than to have them engage us, for we were sure of giving them a drubbing, being in excellent fighting trim, as we were starved and as cross and ill-natured as curs. The British, however, thought better of the matter, and, after several days maneuvering on the hill, very civilly walked off into Philadelphia again.

Starvation seemed to be entailed upon the army and every animal connected with it. The oxen, brought from New England for draught, all died, and the southern horses fared no better; even the wild animals that had any concern with us suffered. A poor little squirrel, who had the ill luck to get cut off from the woods and fixing himself on a tree standing alone and surrounded by several of the soldier's huts, sat upon the tree till he starved to death and fell off the tree. He, however, got rid of his misery soon. He did not live to starve by piecemeal six or seven years. . . .

Soon after the British had quit their position on Chestnut Hill, we left this place and after marching and countermarching back and forward some days, we crossed the Schuylkill in a cold, rainy and snowy night upon a bridge of wagons set end to end and joined together by boards and planks. And after a few days more maneuvering we at last settled down at a place called "the Gulf" (so named on account of a remarkable chasm in the hills); and here we encamped some time, and here we had liked to have encamped forever—for starvation here *rioted* in its glory. But lest the reader should be disgusted at hearing so much said about "starvation," I will give him something that, perhaps, may in some measure alleviate his ill humor.

While we lay here there was a Continental Thanksgiving ordered by Congress; and as the army had all the cause in the world to be particularly thankful, if not for being well off, at least that it was no worse, we were ordered to participate in it. We had nothing to eat for two or three days previous, except what the trees of the fields and forests afforded us. But we must now have what Congress said, a sumptuous Thanksgiving to close the year of high living we had now nearly seen brought to a close. Well, to add something extraordinary to our present stock of provisions, our country, ever mindful of its suffering army, opened her sympathizing heart so wide, upon this occasion, as to give us something to make the world stare. And what do you think it was, reader? Guess. You cannot guess, be you as much of a Yankee as you will. I will tell you; it gave each and every man *half* a *gill*³ of rice and a *tablespoonful* of vinegar!!

After we had made sure of this extraordinary superabundant donation, we were ordered out to attend a meeting and hear a sermon delivered upon the happy occasion. We accordingly went, for we could not help it. I heard a sermon, a "thanksgiving sermon," what sort of one I do not know now, nor did I at the time I heard it. I had something else to think upon. My belly put me in remembrance of the fine Thanksgiving dinner I was to partake of when I could get it. I remember the text, like an attentive lad at church. I can *still* remember that it was this, "And the soldiers said unto him, And what shall we do? And he said unto them, Do violence to no man, nor accuse anyone

3. about four ounces, or half a cup

falsely." The preacher ought to have added the remainder of the sentence to have made it complete, "And be content with your wages." But that would not do, it would be too apropos. However, he heard it as soon as the service was over, it was shouted from a hundred tongues. Well, we had got through the services of the day and had nothing to do but to return in good order to our tents and fare as we could. As we returned to our camp, we passed by our commissary's quarters. All his stores, consisting of a barrel about two-thirds full of hocks of fresh beef, stood directly in our way, but there was a sentinel guarding even that. However, one of my messmates purloined a piece of it, four or five pounds perhaps. I was exceeding glad to see him take it; I thought it might help to eke out our Thanksgiving supper, but alas! how soon my expectations were blasted! The sentinel saw him have it as soon as I did and obliged him to return it to the barrel again. So I had nothing else to do but to go home and make out my supper as usual, upon a leg of nothing and no turnips.

The army was now not only starved but naked. The greatest part were not only shirtless and barefoot, but destitute of all other clothing, especially blankets. I procured a small piece of raw cowhide and made myself a pair of moccasins, which kept my feet (while they lasted) from the frozen ground, although, as I well remember, the hard edges so galled my ankles, while on a march, that it was with much difficulty and pain that I could wear them afterwards; but the only alternative I had was to endure this inconvenience or to go barefoot, as hundreds of my companions had to, till they might be tracked by their blood upon the rough frozen ground. But hunger, nakedness and sore shins were not the only difficulties we had at that time to encounter; we had hard duty to perform and little or no strength to perform it with.

The army continued at and near the Gulf for some days, after which we marched for the Valley Forge in order to take up our winter quarters. We were now in a truly forlorn condition,—no clothing, no provisions and as disheartened as need be. We arrived, however, at our destination a few days before Christmas. Our prospect was indeed dreary. In our miserable condition, to go into the wild woods and build us habitations to *stay* (not to *live*) in, in such a weak, starved and naked condition, was appalling in the highest degree, especially to New Englanders, unaccustomed to such kind of hardships at home. However, there was no remedy, no alternative but this or dispersion. But dispersion, I believe, was not thought of, at least, I did not think of it. We had engaged in the defense of our injured country and were willing, nay, we were determined to persevere as long as such hardships were not altogether intolerable. I had experienced what I thought sufficient of the hardships of a military life the year before. . . . But we were now absolutely in danger of perishing, and that too, in the midst of a plentiful country. We then had but little and often nothing to eat for days together; but now we had nothing and saw no likelihood of any betterment of our condition. Had there fallen deep snows (and it was the time of year to expect them) or even heavy and long rainstorms, the whole army must inevitably have perished. Or had the enemy, strong and well provided as he then was, thought fit to pursue us, our poor emaciated carcasses must have "strewed the plain." But a kind and holy Providence took more notice and better care of us than did the country in whose service we were wearing away our lives by piecemeal.

We arrived at the Valley Forge in the evening. It was dark; there was no water to be found and I was perishing with thirst. I searched for water till I was weary and came to my tent without finding any. Fatigue and thirst, joined with hunger, almost made me desperate. I felt at that instant as if I would have taken victuals or drink from the best friend I had on earth by force. I am not writing fiction, all are sober realities. Just after I arrived at my tent, two soldiers, whom I did not know, passed by. They had some water in their canteens which they told me they had found a good distance off, but could not direct me to the place as it was very dark. I tried to beg a draught of water from them but they were as rigid as Arabs.[4] At length I persuaded them to sell me a drink for three pence, Pennsylvania currency, which was every cent of property I could then call my own, so great was the necessity I was then reduced to.

I lay here two nights and one day and had not a morsel of anything to eat all the time, save half of a small pumpkin, which I cooked by placing it upon a rock, the skin side uppermost, and making a fire upon it. By the time it was heat through I devoured it with as keen an appetite as I should a pie made of it at some other time.

The second evening after our arrival here I was warned to be ready for a two days command. I never heard a summons to duty with so much disgust before or since as I did that. How I could endure two days more fatigue without nourishment of some sort I could not tell, for I heard nothing said about "provisions." However, in the morning at roll call, I was obliged to comply. I went to the parade where I found a considerable number, ordered upon the same business, whatever it was. We were ordered to go to the quartermaster general and receive from him our final orders. We accordingly repaired to his quarters, which was about three miles from camp. Here we understood that our destiny was to go into the country on a foraging expedition, which was nothing more nor less than to procure provisions from the inhabitants for the men in the army and forage for the poor perishing cattle belonging to it, at the point of the bayonet. We stayed at the quartermaster general's quarters till sometime in the afternoon, during which time a beef creature was butchered for us. I well remember what fine stuff it was, it was quite transparent. I thought at that time what an excellent lantern it would make. I was, notwithstanding, very glad to get some of it, bad as it looked. We got, I think, two days allowance of it and some sort of bread kind, I suppose, for I do not re-

4. Prior to the mid–seventeenth century, Muslims, who generally were called Arabs by Westerners, had served as middlemen for most of the trade between Europe and Asia. In 1777 they continued to enjoy a reputation for being sharp traders.

member particularly about that, but it is probable we did. We were then divided into several parties and sent off upon our expedition.

Our party consisted of a lieutenant, a sergeant, a corporal and eighteen privates. We marched till night when we halted and took up our quarters at a large farmhouse. The lieutenant, attended by his waiter, took up his quarters for the night in the hall with the people of the house. We were put into the kitchen. We had a snug room and a comfortable fire, and we began to think about cooking some of our *fat* beef. One of the men proposed to the landlady to sell her a shirt for some sauce. She very readily took the shirt, which was worth a dollar at least. She might have given us a mess of sauce, for I think she would not have suffered poverty by so doing, as she seemed to have a plenty of *all* things. After we had received the sauce, we went to work to cook our supper. By the time it was eatable the family had gone to rest. We saw where the woman went into the cellar, and, she having left us a candle, we took it into our heads that a little good cider would not make our supper relish any the worse; so some of the men took the water pail and drew it full of excellent cider, which did not fail to raise our spirits considerably. Before we lay down the man who sold the shirt, having observed that the landlady had flung it into a closet, took a notion to repossess it again. We marched off early in the morning before the people of the house were stirring, consequently did not know or see the woman's chagrin at having been overreached by the soldiers.

This day we arrived at Milltown, or Downingstown, a small village halfway between Philadelphia and Lancaster, which was to be our quarters for the winter. It was dark when we had finished our day's march. There was a commissary and a wagon master general stationed here, the commissary to take into custody the provisions and forage that we collected, and the wagon master general to regulate the conduct of the wagoners and direct their motions. The next day after our arrival at this place we were put into a small house in which was only one room, in the center of the village. We were immediately furnished with rations of good and wholesome beef and flour, built us up some berths to sleep in, and filled them with straw, and felt as happy as any other pigs that were no better off than ourselves.

A Teenage Girl Describes an Officer's Existence

Sarah Wister

While Private Joseph Plumb Martin and his fellows were scrounging for food and shelter, several officers in the same army were living a different lifestyle. Whenever possible, American officers, especially generals and their staffs, were boarded with local patriot families. While the troops slept in tents and lean-tos, the officers often slept in beds. While the troops struggled to survive on starvation rations, the officers often took their meals at table, often accompanied by a glass or two of wine.

Sarah (Sally) Wister was fifteen years old when her well-to-do family fled Philadelphia in 1776. For the next year her family shared a large farmhouse with the Foulke family in North Wales, about twenty miles north of the city. The farmhouse was not far from Germantown, where a major battle was fought on October 3–4, 1777. Just before and after the battle, a number of American officers boarded with the Wisters and Foulkes. In this excerpt from her journal, Wister describes how exciting it was to be surrounded for a time by gallant, handsome young men. She also sheds light on how different an officer's existence was compared to a private.

As you read, consider the following questions:
1. At the Foulke farmhouse, how did officers live? How did privates live? How do you explain the difference?
2. How might Private Joseph Plumb Martin, author of "A Continental Private Describes a Soldier's Existence," react to Sarah Wister's journal?

Sarah Wister, "The Diary of Sarah Wister," *Weathering the Storm: Women of the American Revolution*, edited by Elizabeth Evans. New York: Charles Scribner's Sons, 1975.

3. How do the adult Wisters and Foulkes react to having soldiers billeted in their house and yard? Do you suppose your parents' reactions would be mostly similar or mostly different? Why?

September 24, 1777: Two Virginia officers called at our house and informed us that the British army had crossed the Schuylkill. Presently after, another person stopped, and confirmed what they had said, and that General Washington and army were near Pottsgrove. Well, thee may be sure we were sufficiently scared; however, the road was very still till evening. About seven o'clock we heard a great noise. To the door we all went. A large number of waggons, with about three hundred of the Philadelphia militia. They begged for drink, and several pushed into the house. One of those that entered was a little tipsy, and had a mind to be saucy. I then thought it time for me to retreat; so figure me (mightily scared, as not having presence of mind enough to face so many of the military) running in at one door and out another, all in a shake with fear; but after a while, seeing the officers appear gentlemanly and the soldiers civil, I called reason to my aid. My fears were in some measure dispelled, tho' my teeth rattled and my hands shook like an aspen leaf. They did not offer to take their quarters with us; so, with many blessings, and as many adieus, they marched off.

Sept. 25: This day, till twelve o'clock, the road was mighty quiet, when Hobson Jones came riding along. He made a stop at our door, and said the British were at Skippack Road, that we should soon see the light horse. A party of Hessians had actually turned into our lane. My dadda and mamma gave it the credit it deserved, for he does not keep strictly to the truth in all respects; but the delicate, chicken-hearted Liddy Foulke and me were wretchedly scared. We could say nothing but "Oh! What shall we do? What will become of us?" These questions only augmented the terror we were in. Well, the fright went off. We seen no light horse or Hessians. Owen Foulke came here in the evening and told us that General Washington had come down as far as the Trappe, and that General McDougle's brigade was stationed at Montgomery, consisting of about 16 hundred men. This he had from Dr. Edwards, Lord Stirling's[1] aide-de-camp; so we expected to be in the midst of one army or t'other.

Sept. 26: We were unusually silent all the morning. No passengers came by the house, except to the mill, and we don't place much dependence on mill news. About 12 o'clock, cousin Jesse heard that General Howe's army had moved down towards Philadelphia. Then, my dear,[2] our hopes and fears were engaged for you. However, my advice is, summon up all your resolution, call Fortitude to your aid, don't suffer your spirits to sink, my dear. There's nothing like courage; 'tis what I stand in need of myself, but unfortunately have but little of it in my composition. I was standing in the kitchen about 12, when somebody came to me in a hurry, screaming, "Sally, Sally, here are the light horse!" This was by far the greatest fright I had endured. Fear tacked wings to my feet. I was at the house in a moment; at the porch I stopt, and it really was the light horse. I run immediately to the western door, where the family were assembled, anxiously waiting for the event. They rode up to the door and halted, and enquired if we had horses to sell. He was answered negatively. "Have not you, sir," to my father, "two black horses?" "Yes, but have no mind to dispose of them." My terror had by this time nearly subsided. The officer and men behaved perfectly civil; the first drank two glasses of wine, rode away, bidding his men follow, which, after adieus in number, they did. The officer was Lieutenant Lindsay of Bland's regiment, Lee's troop. They, to our great joy, were Americans, and but four in all.

1. William Alexander, a general in George Washington's army. Born in New York City, Alexander petitioned the House of Lords to recognize him as the rightful earl of Stirling. His petition was denied, but throughout America he was regarded as Lord Stirling. 2. Debby Norris, Sally's friend in Philadelphia for whom the journal was written

What made us imagine them British, they wore blue and red, which with us is not common. It has rained all this afternoon and, to present appearances, will all night in all probability. The English will take possession of the city [Philadelphia] tomorrow or next day. What a change will it be. May the Almighty take you under His protection, for without His divine aid all human assistance is vain.

May heaven's guardian arm protect my absent friends,
From danger guard them, and from want defend.

Forgive, my dear, the repetition of those lines, but they just darted into my mind. Nothing worth relating has occured this afternoon. Now for trifles. I have set a stocking on the needles, and intend to be mighty industrious. This evening some of our folks heard a very heavy cannon. We suppose it to be fired by the English. The report seemed to come from Philadelphia. We hear the American army will be within five miles of us tonight. The uncertainty of our position engrosses me quite. Perhaps, to be in the midst of war and ruin, and the clang of arms. But we must hope the best. Here, my dear, passes an interval of several weeks in which nothing happened worth the time and paper it would take to write it. The English, however, in the interim, had taken possession of the city.

October 19: Now for new and uncommon scenes. As I was laying in bed and ruminating on past and present events, and thinking how happy I should be if I could see you, Liddy came running into the room and said there was the greatest drumming, fifing, and rattling of waggons that ever she had heard. What to make of this we were at a loss. We dressed and down stairs in a hurry. Our wonder ceased. The British had left Germantown, and our army were marching to take possession. It was the general opinion they would evacuate the capital. Sister Betsy and myself, and George Emlen went about half a mile from home, where we could see the army pass. Thee will stare at my going, but no impropriety, in my opine, or I should not have gone. We made no great stay, but returned with excellent appetites for our breakfast. Several officers called to get some refreshments, but none of consequence till the afternoon. Cousin Prissa and myself were sitting at the door; I in a green skirt, dark short gown. Two genteel men of the military order rode up to the door. "Your servant, ladies," etc.; asked if they could have quarters for General Smallwood.[3] Aunt Foulke thought she could accommodate them as well as most of her neighbors said they could. One of the officers dismounted and wrote "Smallwood's Quarters" over the door, which secured us from straggling soldiers. After this he mounted his steed and rode away. When we were alone our dress and lips were put in order for conquest, and the hopes of adventures gave brightness to each before passive countenance. Thee must be told of a Dr. Gould who, by accident, had made acquantance with my father; a sensible, conversible man, a Carolinian,—and had come to bid us adieu on his going to that state. Daddy had prevailed upon him to stay a day or two with us. In the evening his generalship came with six attendants—which composed his family—a large guard of soldiers, a number of horses and baggage waggons. The yard and house was in confusion and glittered with military equipments. Gould was intimate with Smallwood,[4] and had gone into Jesse's to see him. While he was there, there was great running up and down stairs, so I had an opportunity of seeing and being seen, the former the most agreeable, to be sure. One person in particular attracted my notice. He appeared cross and reserved; but thee shall see how agreeably disappointed I was. Dr. Gould ushered the gentlemen into our parlour, and introduced them. General Smallwood, Captain Furnival, Major Stoddert, Mr. Prig, Captain Finley, and Mr. Clagan, Colonel Wood, and Colonel Line. Those last two did not come with the general. They are Virginians, and both indisposed. The general and suite are Mary-

3. General William Smallwood commanded the Maryland troops in Washington's army.   4. meaning Gould was an acquaintance of Smallwood

landers. Be assured I did not stay long with so many men, but secured a good retreat, heart-safe, so far. Some supped with us, others at Jesse's. They retired about ten, in good order. How new is our situation! I feel in good spirits, though surrounded by an army: the house full of officers, yard alive with soldiers—very peaceable sort of men, tho'. They eat like other folks, talk like them, and behave themselves with elegance; so I will not be afraid of them. That I won't. Adieu. I am going to my chamber to dream, I suppose of bayonets and swords, sashes, guns, and epaulets.

Oct. 20: Morning—I dare say thee is impatient to know my sentiments of the officers; so, while Somnus[5] embraces them, and the house is still, take their characters according to their rank. The general is tall, portly, well-made. A truly martial air, the behaviour and manners of a gentleman, a good understanding, and great humanity of disposition constitute the character of Smallwood. Col. Wood, from what we hear of him and what we see, is one of the most amiable of men: tall and genteel, an agreeable countenance and deportment. The following lines will more fully characterize him.

How skilled he is in each obliging art,
The mildest manners with the bravest heart.

The cause he is fighting for alone tears him from the society of an amiable wife and engaging daughter. With tears in his eyes he often mentions the sweets of domestic life. Col. Line is not married, so let me not be too warm in his praise, lest you suspect. He is monstrous tall and brown, but has a certain something in his face and conversation very agreeable. He entertains the highest notions of honour, is sensible and humane, and a brave officer; he is only seven and twenty years old, but, by a long indisposition and constant fatigue, looks very older and almost worn to a skeleton, but very lively and talkative. Capt. Furnival—I need not

5. sleep

say more of him than that he has, excepting one or two, the handsomest face I ever saw, a very fine person; fine light hair, and a great deal of it, adds to the beauty of his face. Well here comes the glory, the major, so bashful, so famous, he should come before the captain, but never mind. I at first thought the major cross and proud, but I was mistaken. He is about nineteen, nephew to the general, and acts as major of brigade to him; he cannot be extolled for the graces of person, but for those of the mind he may justly be celebrated. He is large in his person, manly, and an engaging countenance and address. Finley is wretched ugly, but he went away last night, so I shall not particularize him. Nothing of any moment today; no acquaintance with the officers. Cols. Wood and Line, and Gould dined with us. I was dressed in my chintz and looked smarter than night before.

Oct. 21: I just now met the major, very reserved: nothing but "Good morning," or "Your servant, madam;" but Furnival is most agreeable; he chats every opportunity; but luckily has a wife. I have heard strange things of the major. Worth a fortune of thirty thousand pounds, independent of anybody, the major moreover is vastly bashful; so much so he can hardly look at the ladies. (Excuse me, good sir; I really thought you were not clever; 'tis bashfulness only, we will drive that away.)

Oct. 25: Evening—Prepare to hear amazing things. The general was invited to dine, was engaged; but Colonel Wood, Major Stoddert, and Dr. Edwards dined with us. In the afternoon, Stoddert, addressing himself to mamma, "Pray, ma'am, do you know Miss Nancy Bond?" I told him of the amiable girl's death. This major had been at Philadelphia College. In the evening I was diverting Johnny[6] at the table, when he drew his chair to it and began to play with the child. I asked him if he knew N. Bond. "No, ma'am, but I have seen her very often." One word brought on another one. We chatted the greatest part of the evening. He

6. Sally's younger brother

said he knew me directly as he seen me. Told me exactly where we lived. It rains now, so adieu.

Oct. 26: A very rainy morning, so like to prove. The officers in the house all day. Afternoon—The general and officers drank tea with us and stayed part of the evening. After supper I went into aunt's, where sat the general, Colonel Line, and Major Stoddert, so Liddy and me seated ourselves at the table in order to read a verse book. The major was holding a candle for the general, who was reading a newspaper. He looked at us, turned away his eyes, looked again, put the candlestick down, up he jumps, out of the door he went. "Well," said I to Liddy, "he will join us when he comes in." Presently he returned, and seated himself on the table. "Pray, ladies, is there any songs in that book?" "Yes, many." "Can't you favor me with a sight of it?" "No, major; 'tis a borrowed book." "Miss Sally, can't you sing?" "No." Thee may be sure I told the truth there. Liddy, saucy girl, told him I could. He begged, and I denied; for my voice is not much better than a raven. We talked and laughed for an hour. He is very clever, amiable, and polite. He has the softest voice, never pronounces the "r" at all.

I must tell thee, today arrived Colonel Gist and Major Leatherberry; the former a smart widower, the latter a lawyer, a sensible young fellow, and will never swing[7] for want of tongue. Dr. Diggs came Second day [Monday]; a mighty disagreeable man. We were obliged to ask him to tea. He must needs prop himself between the major and me, for which I did not thank him. After I had drank tea, I jumped from the table and seated myself at the fire. The major followed my example, drew his chair close to mine, and entertained me very agreeably. Oh Debby, I have a thousand things to tell thee. I shall give thee so droll an account of my adventures that thee will smile. "No occasion of that, Sally," methinks I hear thee say, "for thee tells me every trifle." But, child, thee is mistaken, for I have not told thee half the civil things that are said of us *sweet* creatures

7. be hanged

at "General Smallwood's quarters." I think I might have sent the gentlemen to their chambers. I made my adieus, and home I went.

Oct. 27: Morning—A polite "good morning" from the major, very sociable than ever. No wonder; a stoic could not resist such affable damsels as we are. Evening—We had again the pleasure of the general and suite at afternoon tea. He (the general, I mean) is most agreeable; so lively, so free, and chats so gaily that I had quite an esteem for him. I must steel my heart. Captain Furnival is gone to Baltimore, the residence of his beloved wife. The major and I had a little chat to ourselves this eve. No harm, I assure thee; he and I are friends. This eve came a parson belonging to the army. He is, how shall I describe him, near seven foot high, thin, and meagre, not a single personal charm, very few mental ones. He fell violently in love with Liddy at first sight; the first discovered conquest that has been made since the arrival of the general. Come, shall we chat about Col. Gist? He's very pretty; a charming person. His eyes are exceptional, very stern, and he so rolls them about that mine always fall under them. He bears the character of a brave officer; another admirer of Liddy's, and she of him. When will Sally's admirer's appear? Ah, that indeed. Why, Sally has not charms sufficient to pierce the heart of a soldier. But still I won't dispair. Who knows what mischief I yet may do. Well, Debby, here's Dr. Edwards come again. Now we shall not want clack,[8] for he has a perpetual motion in his head, and if he was not so clever as he is, we should get tired.

Oct. 29: I walked into aunt's this evening. I met the major. Well, thee will think I am writing his history; but not so. Pleased with the encounter, Betsy, Stoddert, and myself, seated by the fire, chatted away an hour in lively and agreeable conversation. I can't pretend to write all he said; but he shone in every subject that was talked of.

Oct. 31: A most charming day. I walked to the door and received the salutation of the morn from Stoddert and other

8. rapid, continuous talk

officers. As often as I go to the door, so often have I seen the major. We chat passingly, as, "A fine day, Miss Sally." "Yes, very fine, major." Night—Another very charming conversation with the young Marylander. He seems possessed of very amiable manners; sensible and agreeable. He has by his unexceptional deportment engaged my esteem.

November 1: Morning—Liddy, Betsy, and a T.L. (prisoner of this state) went to the mill. We made very free with some Continental flour. We were powdered mighty white, to be sure. Home we came. Col. Wood was standing at a window with a young officer. He gave him a push forward, as much as to say, "Observe what fine girls we have here." For all I do not mention Wood as often as he deserves. It is not because we are not sociable; we are very much so, and he is often at our house. Liddy and I had a kind of adventure with him this morn. We were in his chamber chatting about our little affairs, and no idea of being interupted. We were standing up, each an arm on a chest of drawers. The door banged open—Col. Wood was in the room; we started, the colour flew into our faces and crimsoned us over; the tears flew into my eyes. It was very silly, but his coming was so abrupt. He was between us and the door. "Ladies, do not be scared, I only want something from my portmanteau; I beg you not to be disturbed." We ran by him, like two partridges, into mamma's room, threw ourselves into chairs, and reproached each other for being so foolish as to blush and look so silly. I was very much vexed at myself, so was Liddy. The colonel laughed at us, and it blew over. The army had orders to march today [to Whitemarsh]; the regulars accordingly did. General Smallwood had the command of militia at that time, and they being in the rear, were not to leave their encampment until Second day. Observe how militaryish I talk. No wonder, when I am surrounded by people of that order. The general, Colonels Wood, Line, Gist, and Crawford, Majors Stoddert and Leatherberry, dined with us today. After dinner, Liddy, Betsy, and thy smart journaliser put on their bonnets, determined to take a walk. We left the house. I naturally looked back; when behold, the two majors seemed debating whether to follow us or not. Liddy said, "We shall have their attendance;" but I did not think so. They opened the gate and came fast after us. They overtook us about ten poles from home and begged leave to attend us. No fear of a refusal. They inquired where we were going. "To neighbor Roberts's. We will introduce you to his daughters; you us to General Stevens." The affair was concluded, and we shortened the way with lively conversation. Our intention of going to Roberts's was frustrated; the rain that had fallen lately had raised the Wissahickon too high to attempt crossing it on foot. We altered the plan of our ramble, left the road, and walked near two miles thro' the woods. . . .

'Tis nonsense to pretend to recount all that was said; my memory is not so obliging; but it is sufficient that nothing happened during our little excursion but what was very agreeable and entirely consistent with the strictist rules of politeness and decorum. I was vexed a little at tearing my muslin petticoat. I had on my white whim, quite as nice as a First day in town. We returned home safe. Smallwood, Wood, and Stoddert drank tea with us and spent the greater part of the evening. I declare this general is very, very entertaining, so good-natured, so good-humoured; yet so sensible I wonder he is not married. Are there no ladies formed to his taste? Some people, my dear, think that there's no difference between good nature and good humour; but according to my opinion, they differ widely. Good nature consists in a naturally amiable and even disposition, free from all peevishness and fretting. It is accompanied by a natural gracefulness—a manner of doing and saying everything agreeably; in short, it steals the senses and captivates the heart. Good humour consists in being pleased, and who would thank a person for being cheerful if they had nothing to take from them otherways. Good humour is a very agreeable companion for an afternoon, but give me good nature for life. Adieu.

Nov. 3: Morning—Today the militia marches, and the general and officers leave us. High ho. I am very sorry; for when you have been with agreeable people, 'tis impossible not to feel regret when they bid you adieu, perhaps for ever. When they leave us we shall be immured in solitude. The major looks dull. About two o'clock the general and major came to bid us adieu. With daddy and mammy they shook hands very friendly; to us they bowed politely. Our hearts were full. I thought major was affected. "Goodby, Miss Sally," spoken very low. He walked hastily and mounted his horse. They promised to visit us soon. We stood at the door to take a last look, all of us very sober. The major turned his horse's head, and rode back, dismounted. "I have forgot my pistols," passed us, and ran upstairs. He came swiftly back as if wishing, through inclination, to stay; by duty compelled to go. He remounted his horse. "Farewell, ladies, till I see you again," and cantered away. We looked at him till the turn in the road hid him from our sight. "Amiable major," "Clever fellow," "Good young man," was echoed from one to the other. I wonder if we shall ever see him again.

A General's Wife Describes Life in the Midst of Battle

Friederike von Riedesel

Women played important noncombatant roles during the American Revolution. In the absence of medical and quartermaster corps, they served as nurses, cooks, and laundresses. Some, like Molly Pitcher, heroine of the Battle of Monmouth Courthouse in 1778, carried water to thirsty troops in the thick of battle. Although a few also served as prostitutes and the like, most "camp followers," as these women were known, were related by marriage or blood to one or more men in the army they attended.

Friederike Charlotte Louise von Riedesel was the wife of General Baron Friedrich von Riedesel, commander of the German troops assigned to British general John Burgoyne's army. She and her children joined her husband in America in 1777 and witnessed the British surrender at Saratoga. In this excerpt from her journal, she describes the horror of the final days of Burgoyne's campaign. She also sheds light on the roles played by camp followers during a battle.

As you read, consider the following questions:
1. How did women participate in Burgoyne's campaign?
2. What insights does Baroness von Riedesel give as to why and how Burgoyne's army was captured at Saratoga?

Toward evening [of October 9], we at last came to Saratoga, which was only half an hour's march from the

Friederike von Riedesel, *Letters and Journals Relating to the War of the American Revolution, and the Capture of the German Troops at Saratoga.* Translated by William L. Stone. Albany, NY: Joel Munsell, 1867.

place where we had spent the whole day. I was wet through and through by the frequent rains, and was obliged to remain in this condition the entire night, as I had no place whatever where I could change my linen. I, therefore, seated myself before a good fire, and undressed my children; after which, we laid ourselves down together upon some straw. I asked General Phillips,[1] who came up to where we were, why we did not continue our retreat while there was yet time, as my husband had pledged himself to cover it and bring the army through.

"Poor woman," answered he, "I am amazed at you! completely wet through, have you still the courage to wish to go further in this weather! Would that you were only our commanding general! He halts because he is tired, and intends to spend the night here and give us a supper."

In this latter achievement, especially, General Burgoyne was very fond of indulging. He spent half the nights in singing and drinking, and amusing himself with the wife of a commissary, who was his mistress, and who, as well as he, loved champagne.

On the 10th, at seven o'clock in the morning, I drank some tea by way of refreshment; and we now hoped from one moment to another that at last we would again get under way. General Burgoyne, in order to cover our retreat, caused the beautiful houses and mills at Saratoga, belonging to General Schuyler,[2] to be burned. An English officer brought some excellent broth, which he shared with me, as I was not able to refuse his urgent entreaties.

Thereupon we set out upon our march, but only as far as another place not far from where we had started. The greatest misery and the utmost disorder prevailed in the army. The commissaries had forgotten to distribute provisions among the troops. There were cattle enough, but not one had been killed. More than thirty officers came to me, who could endure hunger no longer. I had coffee and tea made

1. William Phillips commanded the British troops under Burgoyne's command.
2. Philip Schuyler was an American general and a field commander at Saratoga.

for them, and divided among them all the provisions with which my carriage was constantly filled; for we had a cook who, although an arrant knave, was fruitful in all expedients, and often in the night crossed small rivers in order to steal from the country people sheep, poultry and pigs. . . .

The whole army clamored for a retreat, and my husband promised to make it possible, provided only that no time was lost. But General Burgoyne, to whom an order[3] had been promised if he brought about a junction with the army of General Howe,[4] could not determine upon this course, and lost every thing by his loitering.

About two o'clock in the afternoon, the firing of cannon and small arms was again heard, and all was alarm and confusion. My husband sent me a message telling me to betake myself forthwith into a house which was not far from there. I seated myself in the calash[5] with my children, and had scarcely driven up to the house when I saw on the opposite side of the Hudson River five or six men with guns, which were aimed at us. Almost involuntarily I threw the children on the bottom of the calash and myself over them. At the same instant the churls fired, and shattered the arm of a poor English soldier behind us, who was already wounded, and was also on the point of retreating into the house.

Immediately after our arrival a frightful cannonade began, principally directed against the house in which we had sought shelter, probably because the enemy believed, from seeing so many people flocking around it, that all the generals made it their headquarters. Alas! it harbored none but wounded soldiers, or women! We were finally obliged to take refuge in a cellar, in which I laid myself down in a corner not far from the door. My children lay down on the earth with their heads upon my lap, and in this manner we passed the entire night. A horrible stench, the cries of the children, and yet more than all this, my own anguish, pre-

3. a knighthood   4. William Howe was commander in chief of the British army in North America, and personally commanded the troops in the vicinity of New York City.   5. a two-horse, four-wheeled carriage with seating inside for four and an outside seat for the driver

vented me from closing my eyes. On the following morning the cannonade again began, but from a different side. I advised all to go out of the cellar for a little while, during which time I would have it cleaned, as otherwise we would all be sick.

They followed my suggestion, and I at once set many hands to work, which was in the highest degree necessary; for the women and children, being afraid to venture forth, had soiled the whole cellar.

After they had all gone out and left me alone, I for the first time surveyed our place of refuge. It consisted of three beautiful cellars, splendidly arched. I proposed that the most dangerously wounded of the officers should be brought into one of them; that the women should remain in another; and that all the rest should stay in the third, which was nearest the entrance. I had just given the cellars a good sweeping, and had fumigated them by sprinkling vinegar on burning coals, and each one had found his place prepared for him—when a fresh and terrible cannonade threw us all once more into alarm. Many persons, who had no right to come in, threw themselves against the door. My children were already under the cellar steps, and we would all have been crushed, if God had not given me strength to place myself before the door, and with extended arms prevent all from coming in; otherwise every one of us would have been severely injured.

Eleven cannon balls went through the house, and we could plainly hear them rolling over our heads. One poor soldier, whose leg they were about to amputate, having been laid upon a table for this purpose, had the other leg taken off by another cannon ball, in the very middle of the operation. His comrades all ran off, and when they again came back they found him in one corner of the room, where he had rolled in his anguish, scarcely breathing. I was more dead than alive, though not so much on account of our own danger as for that which enveloped my husband. . . .

Our cook saw to our meals, but we were in want of water; and in order to quench thirst, I was often obliged to drink wine and give it, also, to the children. It was, moreover, the only thing that my husband could take, which fact so worked upon our faithful Rockel[6] that he said to me one day, "I fear that the general drinks so much wine because he dreads falling into captivity, and is therefore weary of life." The continual danger in which my husband was encompassed was a constant source of anxiety to me. I was the only one of all the women whose husband had not been killed or wounded, and I often said to myself—especially since my husband was placed in such great danger day and night—"Shall I be the only fortunate one?" He never came into the tent at night, but lay outside by the watch fires. This alone was sufficient to have caused his death, as the nights were damp and cold.

As the great scarcity of water continued, we at last found a soldier's wife who had the courage to bring water from the river, for no one else would undertake it, as the enemy shot at the head of every man who approached the river. This woman, however, they never molested; and they told us afterward that they spared her on account of her sex.

I endeavored to divert my mind from my troubles by constantly busying myself with the wounded. I made them tea and coffee, and received in return a thousand benedictions. Often, also, I shared my noonday meal with them. One day a Canadian officer came into our cellar who could scarcely stand up. We at last got it out of him that he was almost dead with hunger. I considered myself very fortunate to have it in my power to offer him my mess.[7] This gave him renewed strength, and gained for me his friendship. Afterward, upon our return to Canada, I learned to know his family. One of our greatest annoyances was the stench of the wounds. . . .

In this horrible situation we remained six days. Finally, they spoke of capitulating, as by temporizing for so long a time our retreat had been cut off. A cessation of hostilities took place, and my husband, who was thoroughly worn out, was able, for the first time in a long while, to lie down

6. General von Riedesel's valet   7. food

upon a bed. In order that his rest might not be in the least disturbed, I had a good bed made up for him in a little room; while I, with my children and both my maids, lay down in a little parlor close by. But about one o'clock in the night some one came and asked to speak to him. It was with the greatest reluctance that I found myself obliged to awaken him. I observed that the message did not please him, as he immediately sent the man back to headquarters and laid himself down again considerably out of humor.

Soon after this General Burgoyne requested the presence of all the generals and staff officers at a council of war, which was to be held early the next morning; in which he proposed to break the capitulation, already made with the enemy, in consequence of some false information just received. It was, however, finally decided that this was neither practicable nor advisable; and this was fortunate for us, as the Americans said to us afterwards that had the capitulation been broken we all would have been massacred. . . .

At last my husband sent to me a groom with a message that I should come to him with our children. I, therefore, again seated myself in my dear calash; and in the passage through the American camp I observed with great satisfaction that no one cast at us scornful glances. On the contrary, they all greeted me, even showing compassion on their countenances at seeing a mother with her little children in such a situation. I confess that I feared to come into the enemy's camp, as the thing was so entirely new to me.

When I approached the tents, a noble-looking man came toward me, took the children out of the wagon, embraced and kissed them, and then with tears in his eyes helped me also to alight. "You tremble," said he to me. "Fear nothing."

"No," replied I, "for you are so kind, and have been so tender toward my children, that it has inspired me with courage."

He then led me to the tent of General Gates,[8] with whom

8. General Horatio Gates was commander of the Continental army's Northern Department and the general who defeated Burgoyne at Saratoga.

I found Generals Burgoyne and Phillips, who were upon an extremely friendly footing with him.

Burgoyne said to me, "You may now dismiss all your apprehensions, for your sufferings are at an end." I answered him that I should certainly be acting very wrongly to have any more anxiety when our chief had none, and especially when I saw him on such friendly footing with General Gates. All the generals remained to dine with General Gates.

The man who had received me so kindly came up and said to me, "It may be embarrassing to you to dine with all these gentlemen; come now with your children into my tent, where I will give you, it is true, a frugal meal, but one that will be accompanied by the best of wishes."

"You are certainly," answered I, "a husband and a father, since you show me so much kindness."

I then learned that he was the American General Schuyler. He entertained me with excellent smoked tongue, beefsteaks, potatoes, good butter and bread. Never have I eaten a better meal. I was content. I saw that all around me were so likewise; but that which rejoiced me more than every thing else was that my husband was out of all danger. As soon as we had finished dinner, he invited me to take up my residence at his house, which was situated in Albany, and told me that General Burgoyne would, also, be there. I sent and asked my husband what I should do. He sent me word to accept the invitation; and as it was two days' journey from where we were, and already five o'clock in the afternoon, he advised me to set out in advance, and to stay over night at a place distant about three hours' ride. General Schuyler was so obliging as to send with me a French officer, who was a very agreeable man and commanded those troops who composed the reconnoitering party of which I have before made mention. . . .

The day after this we arrived at Albany, where we had so often longed to be. But we came not, as we supposed we should, as victors! We were, nevertheless, received in the most friendly manner by the good General Schuyler, and by his wife and daughters, who showed us the most marked courtesy, as, also, General Burgoyne, although he had—without any necessity it was said—caused their magnificently built houses to be burned. But they treated us as people who knew how to forget their own losses in the misfortunes of others.

Even General Burgoyne was deeply moved at their magnanimity and said to General Schuyler, "Is it to *me*, who have done you so much injury, that you show so much kindness!"

"That is the fate of war," replied the brave man; "let us say no more about it."

We remained three days with them, and they acted as if they were very reluctant to let us go.

A Loyalist Describes His Persecution by the Patriots

Joel Stone

While the Continental and British armies battled one another for control of America, patriots and loyalists fought just as bitterly for control of their local communities. In those areas where the patriots held sway, they harassed anyone in their communities whom they suspected of remaining loyal to the British Crown. In order to convert or neutralize loyalists, or Tories as they were disparagingly called, patriots threatened them with the seizure and sale of their property and the destruction of their homes. When these measures failed, patriots resorted to physical harassment, imprisonment, and even death. In areas that were controlled by loyalists, as New York City and its environs were for almost the entire war, loyalists used the same tactics against patriots.

Joel Stone was a Connecticut man of means and social standing who remained loyal to the king of England. Following the war, he fled the United States and settled in Ontario, Canada, as did thousands of other loyalists. In this selection, he describes how he was harassed by the patriots both before and after he joined a loyalist unit of the British army.

As you read, consider the following questions:
1. Was Stone's treatment by the patriots legal? Was it in keeping with the principles embodied in the Declaration of Independence and the Bill of Rights?
2. Was Stone's treatment in keeping with sound military principles?

Joel Stone, "The Narrative of Joel Stone of Connecticut, 1776–1778," *Loyalist Narratives from Upper Canada*, edited by James Talman. Toronto: The Champlain Society, 1946.

3. Based on Stone's narrative, which should take precedence during a time of war: individual liberty or collective security?

In the year 1776 I discovered that it was perfectly impracticable any longer to conceal my sentiments from the violent public. The agents of Congress acted with all the cunning and cruelty of inquisitors and peremptorily urged me to declare without further hesitation whether I would immediately take up arms against the British Government or procure a substitute to serve in the general insurrection.

I could no longer withhold any positive reply and unalterable resolution of declining to fulfil their request by joining in an act which I actually detested and which had been repeatedly deemed a rebellion by the public proclamation of General Howe.[1] The leader of the faction then informed me that my conduct in consequence of such refusal would undergo the strictest scrutiny and that I might expect to meet the utmost severity to my person from those in authority and an incensed public.

Thus perpetually perplexed and harassed, I determined in my own mind to withdraw as soon as possible to the City of New York and thereby joining his Majesty's forces cast what weight I was able into the opposite scale. But before I could carry my design into execution a warrant by order of the agents of Congress[2] was issued out in order to seize my person. Being apprized of this and hearing that a party of men were actually on their way to my house, I packed up my books and bills, which I delivered to a careful friend to secrete, and left the care of my effects in the house to one of my sisters who had lived with me some time. Before the tumultuous mob which attended the party surrounded the premises, I had the good fortune to get

1. General William Howe, commander in chief of the British army sent to New York City in 1776 to quell the American Revolution 2. the Second Continental Congress, which oversaw American resistance to the British for the duration of the American Revolution

away on horseback and, being in the dark night, happily eluded their search. But my sister, as I was afterwards given to understand, met the resentment of the mob, who from language the most opprobrious proceeded to actual violence, breaking open every lock in the house and seizing all the property they could discover. My goods and chattels thus confiscated they exposed to sale as soon as possible in opposition to the repeated remonstrances of my partner, declaring that the whole estate, real and personal, was become the property of the States.

But I soon found that my person was one principal object of their aim. Being informed to what place I had fled, a party of about twelve armed men with a constable came up and, seizing my horse, were proceeding into the house when I found an opportunity to slip from their hands. [It] was full fourteen days before I was perfectly secure, during which time several parties were detached after me, whom they were taught to consider as a traitor to the United States and unworthy to live. An invincible frenzy appeared to pervade the minds of the country people, and those very men who so recently had held one in the highest esteem became the most implacable enemies. I could not help considering my fate as peculiarly hard in thus being hunted as a common criminal and proscribed without cause in the very country that gave me birth, merely for performing my duty and asserting the rights of the British Constitution.

However, I had the unspeakable happiness to escape the utmost vigilance of my pursuers and at length reached Long Island. There I soon joined the King's army as a volunteer, in company with several gentlemen in the same persecuted situation, who also like myself had missed no opportunity of serving the royal cause but whose execution had been greatly curbed by the popular party. I remained thus until the 15th April, 1778, when, finding my money just expended amidst so many enormous calls and dreading that the patience of my best friends would not hold out much longer however willing they had been to assist me, I accepted a warrant to raise a company (as stated in my memorial presented to the Right Honorable the Lords Commissioners of His Majesty's Treasury), with a view to be in pay, especially as but little prospect was presented of a speedy termination being put to the unhappy war.

On the night of the 12th of May, 1778, as I was lying at Huntington on Long Island in order to carry my purpose of recruiting further into execution, I was surprised while asleep by a company of whale boatmen[3] who took me prisoner and carried [me] over to Norwalk in Connecticut.

The magistrate before whom I was taken refused to consider me as a prisoner of war, which I claimed as a right, but charging me with the enormous crime of high treason against the States I was committed a close prisoner to Fairfield jail. I was there indicted, threatened with the vengeance of the law and warned solemnly for that death which most certainly would be inflicted upon me.

In a situation so perfectly horrible, perpetually exposed to the most barbarous insults of the populace and even some of the magistrates of the place, it may easily be supposed I would mediate [meditate] a recovery from a captivity so much to be dreaded. For a purpose so truly desirable I resolved to exert every effort of ingenuity that my mind could suggest. By the aid of my brother and other friends in that country I sent a flag[4] to the commander of the king's army at or nigh King's Bridge in New York, soliciting immediate relief. This not producing the desired effect, I petitioned the Governor . . . that I might . . . be deemed a prisoner of war, treated as such and be permitted to appear before himself and Council in person to remove every objection to the late request. I freely offered to defray all the incidental expences occasioned by my removal across the country. However, he hesitated some time but at last agreed to my proposal. I paid for the strong guard which attended me by the way and entertained some hope of my meeting a favorable reception from the Governor.

3. Throughout the American Revolution, patriots from Connecticut and loyalists on Long Island raided each other by crossing Long Island Sound in whaleboats, long narrow rowboats that handled well in rough seas.   4. a message

The result turned out quite contrary to my wish. My petition was rejected with the utmost disdain and I was reminded to prepare for that approaching fate which was irrevocably fixed, as I was afterwards informed by a decree which could not be thwarted.

On my return the captain and guard buoyed me up by the way with a distant view of clemency, which in a great measure prevented me from an attempt which by the aid of pecuniary means must have freed me from so dreadful a situation, as I discovered that these mercenaries were far from being invulnerable in the respect alluded to. But as that must have cost me a considerable sum, the notion that I should one day be exchanged soothed for the present my perturbed mind and prevented my immediate attempt to escape. But on my return to prison all my sanguine hopes vanished and left my mind in the utmost agitation. I began to renew my contrivances and intrigues in conjunction with my friends and resolved to spare no expense in my power to regain my liberty. Many of my schemes, though they cost large sums, proved unsuccessful, yet I did not despair of gaining my point. The dungeon was truly dismal, the walls strong and the place perpetually guarded, yet being in the prime of life my spirits were warm and my passions violent. I therefore firmly determined to effect an escape if I even should be obliged to sink the last shilling and go out naked into the world. . . .

By the generous aid of my friends and a judicious application of almost all the money I could raise [I] happily emerged from that place of horror July 23, 1778, and with quick despatch pursued our way into the wilderness of that country to wait the further assistance of our friends.

A Pennsylvania Woman Describes Her Fear of Both Armies

Margaret Hill Morris

No area was more affected by the American Revolution than those parts of New Jersey and Pennsylvania that lay between New York City and Philadelphia. From 1776 to 1778 this region was the major battleground of the war, and the British and their Hessian allies ravaged the area in search of supplies and rebels alike. To make matters worse, many residents were Quakers who did not believe in war, and the degree of their loyalty to the Revolution was always suspected by the patriots. Consequently, the people of this region had much to fear from both sides.

Margaret Hill Morris was a twenty-nine-year-old Quaker widow. She lived with the family of her married sister, Sarah Dillwyn, in Burlington, New Jersey, about twenty miles up the Delaware River from Philadelphia. Morris began keeping a diary on December 6, 1776, the same day that British troops entered New Brunswick, New Jersey, about thirty-five miles from Burlington. In this excerpt from her diary, she describes the fear that many Americans felt whenever troops of either army came into their communities. She also suggests that most of the people in her community did not care who won the war, so long as their loved ones remained unharmed.

As you read, consider the following questions:
1. Who posed the greater threat to the good people of Burlington, the Hessians or the patriots? Why?

Margaret Hill Morris, "The Diary of Margaret Hill Morris," *Weathering the Storm: Women of the American Revolution*, edited by Elizabeth Evans. New York: Charles Scribner's Sons, 1975.

2. Do the patriots in this selection bear any resemblance to the ones in "A Loyalist Describes His Persecution by the Patriots"? If so, why? If not, why not?

December 6, 1776: Being on a visit to Haddonfield,[1] I was preparing to return to my family, when a person from Philadelphia told us the people were in great commotion, that the English fleet was in the river, and hourly expected to sail up to the city; that the inhabitants were removing into the country; and that several persons of considerable repute had been discovered to have formed a design of setting fire to the city, and were summoned before the congress and strictly enjoined to drop the horrid purpose. When I heard the above report my heart almost died within me, and I cried that surely the Lord will not punish the innocent with the guilty, that I wished there might be found some interceding Lots and Abrahams amongst *our people*. On my journey home I was told the inhabitants of our little town were going in haste into the country, and that my nearest neighbors were already removed. When I heard this I felt myself quite sick; I was ready to faint. I thought of my Sarah Dillwyn (the beloved companion of my widowed state)—her husband at the distance of some hundred miles from her. I thought of my own lonely situation, no husband to cheer with the voice of love my sinking spirits. My little flock, too, without a father to direct them how to steer. All these things crowded into my mind at once, and I felt like one forsaken. A flood of friendly tears came to my relief, and I felt a humble confidence that He who had been with me in six troubles[2] would not forsake me now. While I cherished this hope, my tranquility was restored, and I felt no sensations but of humble acquiescence to the Divine will. I was favoured to find my family in good health on my

1. Haddonfield, New Jersey, which is not far from Philadelphia and about twenty miles from Burlington   2. the deaths of six close relatives, including a son and her husband

arrival, and my dear companion not greatly discomposed, for which favour I desire to be made truly thankful.

Dec. 7: A letter from my next neighbour's husband, at the camp, warned her to be gone in haste. Many persons coming into town today brought intelligence that the British army were advancing towards us.

Dec. 8: Every day begins and ends with the same accounts. We hear today that the regulars [British] are at Trenton. Some of our neighbours gone, and others going, makes our little bank look lonesome. But our trust in Providence still firm, and we dare not even talk of removing our family.

Dec. 9: This evening we were favoured with the company of our faithful friend and brother, Richard Wells [husband of Margaret's sister Rachel]. This testimony of his love was truly acceptable to us.

Dec. 10: Today our amiable friend Hetty Cox and her family bid us adieu. My brother also left us, but returned in less than an hour, telling us he could not go away just as the Hessians were entering the town. But, with no troops coming in, we urged him to leave us next morning, which he concluded to do, after preparing us to expect the Hessians in a few hours. A number of galleys [double-masted boats commanded by Commodore Thomas Seymour of the Pennsylvania Navy] had been lying in the river before the town, for two days past.

Dec. 11: After various reports from one hour to another of light-horse approaching, the people in town had certain intelligence that a large body of Hessians were come to Bordentown, and we might expect to see them in a few hours. About 10 o'clock of this day a party of about 60 men [Pennsylvania riflemen] marched down Main Street. As they passed along they told our doctor [Jonathan Odell, an Episcopal clergyman and doctor] and some other persons in the town that a large number of Hessians were advancing, and would be in the town in less than an hour. This party were riflemen who, it seems, had crossed the river somewhere in the neighbourhood of Bordentown to reconnoitre, and meeting with a superior number of Hessians on the road, were then returning, and took Burlington on their way back; from us they crossed to Bristol, and by the time they were fairly embarked, the Hessians—to the number, as we heard, of 4 or 500—had passed what we call York Bridge. On the first certainty of their approach, John Lawrence and two or three others thought it best for the safety of the town to go out and meet the troops. He communicated his intention to one of the gondola [smaller boat in Seymour's fleet] captains, who approved of it and desired to be informed of the result. The gentlemen went out, and though the Hessian colonel spoke but little English, yet they found that upon being thus met in a peaceable manner on behalf of the inhabitants, he was ready to promise them safety and security, to exchange any messages that might be proper with the gentlemen of the galleys. In the meantime he ordered his troops to halt; they remained in their ranks between the Bridge and the corner of Main Street, waiting an answer from on board. John Lawrence and T. Hulings went down to report what had passed, and told Capt. Moore that the colonel had orders to quarter his troops in Burlington that night, and that if the inhabitants were quiet and peaceable, and would furnish him with quarters and refreshment, he would pledge his honor that no manner of disorder should happen to disturb or alarm the people. Capt. Moore replied that in his opinion it would be wrong in such a case to fire on the town, but that he would go down and consult the commodore, and return an answer as soon as might be. While this answer was waited for, Dr. Odell was told it would be a satisfaction, both to the Hessian commandant and to our own people, to have a person who could serve as interpreter between them. Not doubting the foreigner could speak French, the doctor went to him, and he had the satisfaction to find it probable, at least, that he might be of service to the people of the town. The commandant seemed highly pleased to find a person with whom he could converse with ease and precision. He desired the doctor to tell the gentlemen of the town to the same purport as above, with this addition: that he expected there would be found no persons in the town in arms; nor any arms, ammunition, or other effects, belonging to persons that were in arms against the king, concealed by any of the inhabitants; that if any such effects were thus secreted, the house in which they should be found would be given up to pillage; to prevent which, it would be necessary to give him a just and fair account of such effects, which account he would forward to the general, and that if we acted openly and in good faith in these respects, he repeated his assurances, upon the honour of a soldier, that he would be answerable for every kind of disorder on the part of his troops. They remained in profound silence in their ranks, and the commandant with some of his officers came into town as far as John Lawrence's, where they dined, waiting the commodore's answer. The doctor says, that as he thought he observed much of the gentleman in the commandant, and the appearance, at least, of generosity and humanity, he took an opportunity to inform him that there was an old friend of his [the doctor's] who was a colonel, and of some estimation in the Continental Army—that he was at present with Gen. Washington; that his lady, an amiable woman, had gone into the country with most of her effects; that the doctor was ignorant of the place of her retreat, but that before her departure she had begged him on the footing of former friendship to take into his house, and if he might be permitted to keep as under his protection, some few things which she could not remove, and told the commandant, he was ready to give an exact account of such of her effects as he had thus taken charge of. At the same time, he confessed that when he took them it was in the hope of being suffered to preserve them for his friend. The commandant told him without a moment's hesitation, "Sir, you need not be at the trouble of giving any further account of those things you have so candidly mentioned. Be assured that whatever effects have been entrusted with you in this way, I shall consider as your own, and they shall not be touched." From this answer he was encouraged to hope he might be of still further service to his friends, in the full persuasion that nothing would happen to disconcert the peaceable disposition that was making. But as it happened, the commodore had received intelligence of a party of Hessians having entered Burlington, before Capt. Moore got down to him, and had ordered up four galleys to fire on the town wherever any two or three persons should be seen together. Capt. Moore met and hailed them, one after another, but the wind was so high that he was not heard or understood. The four gondolas came up; the first of them appearing before Main Street. John Lawrence, T. Hulings and William Dillwyn went down upon the wharf and waved a hat, the signal agreed on with Capt. Moore for the boat to come ashore and give the commodore's answer in peace. To the astonishment of these gentlemen, all the answer they received was first a swivel shot. Not believing it possible this could be designedly done, they stood still, and John Lawrence again waved his hat, and was answered with an 18 pounder. Both these fires, as the gondola people have since told us, were made with as good aim as could be taken, as they took it for granted it was at Hessians they fired. However, as it was impossible to conjecture how such conduct could have happened, or to suspect such a mistake, 'tis no wonder the town was exceedingly alarmed, looking upon it in the light of a cruel as well as unprovoked piece of treachery. Upon this news the commandant rose calmly from table, his officers with him, and went out to eight or ten men who had come to the door as a bodyguard. He turned to the doctor as he went into the street, and said he could easily dispose of his people out of the possibility of danger, but that much mischief might be done to the town, and that he would take a view of the gondolas and see what measures might be necessary on his part; but that he should be sorry to be the occasion of any damage or distress to the inhabitants. He walked down the street, and sent different ways three sentinels in Indian file together—to view and report to him what they saw. These being now and then seen at different times in divers parts of the town, induced the people on board to believe that the houses were full of Hessians. A cannonade was continued till almost dark in different directions, sometimes along the street, sometimes across it. Several houses were struck and a little damaged, but not one living creature, either man or beast, killed or wounded. About dark the gondolas fell down a little way below the town, and the night was passed in quiet. While all this tumult was in town we, on our peaceful bank, ignorant of the occasion of the firing, were wondering what it could mean, and unsuspecting of danger, were quietly pursuing our business in the family, when a kind neighbour informed us of the occasion, and urged us to go into the cellar as a place of safety. We were prevailed on by him to do so, and remained there till it ceased.

Dec. 12: The people of the galleys, suspecting that some troops were yet either concealed in town or in the neighborhood of it, have been very jealous of the inhabitants, who have been often alarmed with reports that the city [Philadelphia] would be set on fire. Many have gone in haste and great distress into the country, but we still hope no mischief is seriously intended. A number of men landed on our bank this morning, and told us it was their settled purpose to set fire to the town. I begged them not to set my house afire. They asked which was my house. I showed it to them, and they said they knew not what hindered them from firing on it last night, for seeing a light in the chambers they thought there were Hessians in it, and they pointed the guns at it several times. I told them my children were sick, which obliged me to burn a light all night. Though they did not know what hindered them from firing on us, I did. It was the guardian of the widow and the orphan, who took us into His safekeeping, and preserved us from danger. Oh, that I may keep humble, and be thankful for this, as well as other favours vouchsafed to my little flock.

Dec. 13: This day we began to look a little like ourselves again. The troops were removed some miles from town, as we heard, and our friends began to venture out to see us. But the suspicions of the gondola men still continued, and search was made in and about the town for men distinguished by the name of Tories.[3] About noon of this day dear brother Richard Wells popped in upon us. He heard the firing yesterday, and being anxious for our safety, he ran the risk of venturing amongst us to see how we had fared. Surely this proof of his love will never be forgotten by me while my memory lasts. He left us soon after dinner.

Dec. 14: This day we began to feel a little like ourselves again. This day there was no appearance of the formidable Hessians. Our friends began to show themselves abroad. Several called to see us; amongst the number was one (Dr. Odell) esteemed by the whole family, and *very intimate* in it; but the spirit of the devil still continued to rove through the town in the shape of Tory-hunters. A message was delivered to our intimate friend, informing him a party of armed men were on the search for him—his horse was brought, and he retired to a place of safety. Some of the gentlemen who entertained the foreigners were pointed out to the gondola men. Two worthy inhabitants were seized upon and dragged on board. From the 13th to the 16th we had various reports of the advancing and retiring of the enemy. Parties of armed men rudely entered the houses in town, and a diligent search was made for Tories. Some of the gondola gentry broke into and pillaged Richard Smith's house on the bank. About noon this day (the 16th) a very terrible account of thousands coming into town [500 New Jersey militia and artillerymen] and now actually to be seen on Gallows Hill. My incautious son caught up the spyglass, and was running towards the mill to look at them. I told him it would be liable to misconstruction, but he prevailed on me to let him gratify his curiosity. He went, but returned much dissatisfied, for no troops could he see. As he came back poor Dick took the glass and, resting it against a tree, took a view of the fleet. Both of these were observed by the people on board, who suspected it was an enemy that was watching their motions. They manned a boat, and sent her on shore. A loud knocking on my door brought me to it. I

3. loyalists

was a little fluttered and kept locking and unlocking that I might get my ruffled face a little composed. At last I opened it, and half a dozen men, all armed, demanded the keys of the empty house. I asked what they wanted there; they said to search for a d——d Tory who had been spying at them from the mill. The name of a Tory, so near to *my own door* seriously alarmed me, for a poor refugee [Dr. Jonathan Odell], dignified by that name, had claimed the shelter of my roof, and was at that very time concealed, like a thief in an auger hole. I rung the bell violently—the signal agreed on if they came to search—and when I thought he had crept into the hole, I put on a very simple look, and cried out "Bless me, I hope you are not Hessians. Say, good men are you the Hessians?" "Do we look like Hessians," asked one of them rudely. "Indeed I don't know." "Did you never see a Hessian?" "No, never in my life; but they are *men*, and you are men, and may be Hessians, for anything I know. But I'll go with you into Col. Cox's house, though indeed it was my son at the mill. He is but a boy, and meant no harm. He wanted to see the troops." So I marched at the head of them, opened the door, and searched every place; but we could not find the Tory—strange where he could be. We returned—they, greatly disappointed—I, pleased to think *my house* was not suspected. The captain, a smart little fellow named Shippen, said he wished he could see the spyglass. Sarah Dillwyn produced it, and very civilly desired his acceptance of it, which I was sorry for, as I often amused myself in looking through it. They left us, and searched James Verree's and the next two houses, but no Tory could they find. This transaction reached the town, and Col. Cox was very angry and ordered the men on board. In the evening I went to town with my refugee and placed him in other lodgings. I was told today of a design to seize upon a young man in town, as he was deemed a Tory. I thought a hint would be kindly received and, as I came back, called on a friend of his, and told him. Next day he was out of the reach of the gondolas.

Dec. 17: More news, great news—very great news. The

British troops are actually at Mount Holly. Guards of militia are placed at London and York bridges. Gondola men in arms are patrolling the street, and a diligent search made for firearms, ammunition, and Tories. Another attempt last night to get into R. Smith's house. Early this morning James Verree sent in, to beg I would let my son go a few miles out of town on some business for him. I consented, not knowing of the formidible doings up town. When I heard of it I felt a mother's pangs for her son all the day. When night came and he did not appear, I made no doubt of his being taken by the Hessians. A friend made my mind easy by telling me he had himself passed through the town where the dreadful Hessians were said to be playing the very mischief. It is certain there were numbers of them at Mount Holly, but they behaved very civilly to the people, excepting only a few persons who were in actual rebellion, as they termed it, whose goods and all they injured. This evening every gondola man was sent on board with strict orders not to set a foot on the Jersey shore again—so far so good.

Dec. 18: This morning gives us hope of a quiet day—but my mind is still anxious for my son, not yet returned. Our refugee has gone off today out of the reach of gondolas and Tory-hunters. Much talk of the enemy. Two Hessians had the assurance to appear in town today; they asked if there were any rebels in town, and desired to be shown the *men-of-war* [warships]—what a burlesque on *men-of-war!* My son returned at night, and to his mortification saw not one Hessian, light-horse, or anything else worth seeing, but had the consolation of a little adventure at York Bridge, being made to give an account of himself as he went out yesterday, his horse detained, and he ordered to walk back to town and get a pass from Gen. Reed [Col. Joseph Reed, Washington's adjutant general]. This he readily agreed to; but instead of a pass, Col. Cox accompanied him back to the bridge, and Don Quixote, jr. mounted his horse and rode through their ranks in triumph.

A British Lieutenant Describes the Hardships of War on Civilians

John Enys

Toward the end of the war, both sides began treating each other with greater ferocity. In the Carolinas, where most of the fighting took place in the 1780s, loyalists and patriots gave and expected no quarter, and prisoners were often put to the sword. Similar occurrences took place on the out-skirts of New York City and other places where either the British army or loyalist militias were strong.

John Enys was a lieutenant with the British Twenty-Ninth Regiment, and was stationed for most of the war in Canada. In 1780 he was part of a group of British regulars, loyalists and Indians that raided Vermont. In this selection from his journal, he describes the mercilessness with which the raiders treated the property of civilians.

As you read, consider the following questions:
1. In your opinion, what was the primary purpose of the raid?
2. In your opinion, did the raiders conduct themselves ap-propriately, given that there was a war going on? If so, why? If not, why not?

On the *6th* about 11 o'clock in the day we crossed the lake[1] and landed a little way above Chimney Point, from whence

1. Lake Champlain

John Enys, *The American Journals of Lt. John Enys*. New York: Syracuse University Press, 1976.

two detachments were ordered, one commanded by Capt. Ross of the 31st Regt consisting of 100 soldiers and all the savages[2] but 6 or 8 who remained with Major Carleton, and the other under the command of Lt. Forquhar of our Regt. The latter was to destroy a mill and some houses near Ticonderoga, and the former of which I was one were to march through the woods to Otter Creek in order to burn and destroy that settlement. About one o'clock both parties marched. We continued until it was very near dark. Marching nearly due east, we arrived at a deep valley surrounded on every side by very high hills so that our fires could not well be discoverd. Here the savages agreed to pass the night. Next morn we marched at daylight and after having marched about 5 miles we came to a pretty large creek. . . . We passed this by means of a large tree fallen across it as it was by no means fordable at this place. A very short distance from the place we crossed this creek we found a large trunk broke open and some empty flour barrels. From this we continued our route about 4 miles further when we came to two small houses, one of which was a blacksmith's shop, but found nobody in either of them, although there was a very good stock of corn, and one horse left. After we had destroy'd these houses we proceded two miles further, when we came to another house which from the furniture must have been a weaver's. Here were also two very large barns well stocked with all sorts of grain. This place did not stop us at all as an advanced guard appointed to burn all they could see had totally destroyed this place before our rear came up. So continuing our march about twelve o'clock we came in upon Otter Creek at a place called Bladgets House, in the upper part of the township of Middlebury.[3] At this place we found only a very small house and barn with a very little corn and no inhabitants.

From hence two detachments were sent out, one under Lt. Houghton of the 53d Regt composed of savages and royalists,[4] to burn a farm house about two miles up the

2. Indian allies of the British   3. Middlebury, Vermont   4. loyalists

creek at which they found a large quantity of grain but neither cattle nor inhabitants. The other was commanded by a French interpreter, one La Motte, and consisted of only 6 or 7 of the upper country Indians, who swam across the creek and burnt a farm or two on the other side but found neither inhabitants nor cattle. The main body waited here for the return of the above parties who were no sooner come in than we proceeded and burnt a great many houses, barns &c. and a very great quantity of hay, corn &c. &c. but found neither cattle nor inhabitants in the course of this day. After we had quit the village if it may be called so as the houses are ½ a mile or a mile sunder, our guide I know not for what reason thought proper to quit the direct road and struck into the woods. After having marched near 5 miles we found ourselves at the house we had burnt in the morning which I before mentioned to have been a blacksmith's shop. After this we were a long while before we gained the proper path again and when we did the day was so far advanced that we got but a very little way forward in the course of our afternoon's marching although we had gone over a great deal of ground.

This evening we encamped a short distance from the ford at which we were to pass the creek. Next morning we moved early and about 7 or 8 o'clock arrived at the ford which the Indians immediately passed and began so warm a fire[5] upon the cattle and poultry that most of us who were in the rear imagined they had been attacked in the passage. We all crossed the ford as fast as we came up. Here for the first time we found inhabitants, who appeared very glad to see the soldiers cross the ford as the savages had frightened them almost to death before our arrival. The family we found here consisted of one man, two women and eight or nine small children.

You can hardly suppose how quietly all these Yankees take any distresses, so much so that they appear to have

5. i.e., the Indians began shooting at the cattle and poultry

lost all sort of feeling. They expressed no sort of surprise or grief at our coming and only said very cooly they did not suppose we should have come so far into their country. One of them appeared a little destressed however when she was told that her husband was to be carried into Canada and that she herself must return to [her] friends higher up the creek or indeed where she chose, so [long as] she did not attempt following her husband which would not be permitted. She said it was very hard to be treated so when they had never done anything against the King's troops which by the bye I believe to be a d———d lie as from all appearance the house was fitted up as a place of defence to command the passage of the ford. At this place was found great plenty of cattle of all kinds, hay, corn, Indian corn, flax and many other things. The inhabitants were suffered to take a certain quantity of every thing necessary for their journey to the first settlement, after which the savages were admitted to plunder the house, a thing they always look upon as their undoubted right. . . . There were also left here a small proportion of provisions of different kinds and one cow to give milk to the children on their passage for which indulgence the woman promised to wait some time for the rest of the inhabitants coming up and to give them all a share of the things which were left.

After we had destroyed all that was here except what I mentioned to be left, and were about to proceed, an account came to us that there were some rebels in a house a little way down on the opposite side of the creek. . . . Lt. Arburthnot of the 31st Regt with 30 men and some savages repassed the ford but on their arrival at the house mentioned found none but the family. Meanwhile after having collected all the cattle we could find and sent them off before us we proceeded down the creek to opposite where Lt. Arburthnot's party were, at which place we burnt another house and waited until his party had destroyed all on the other side of the water and crossed which was effected by means of a canoe found at that place. Our whole party being joined again we proceeded down the creek burning and destroying all we found until near dark when we encamped at a mile or two's distant from the lower falls. It would be endless to mention every house that was destroy'd this day, nor could I do it if I was inclined as I do not know the number.

4

COMPLETING THE REVOLUTION

CHAPTER PREFACE

Having decided on independence, the Americans also had to decide how to govern themselves. Their answer was to formalize the type of government that had existed informally in the colonies for years. By 1777 all thirteen colonies had adopted state constitutions; most duplicated the situation in the colonies before independence by establishing a two-house legislature and a weak governor. That same year the thirteen states attempted to ally themselves militarily by drawing up the Articles of Confederation. The articles, which were not ratified until 1781, put most power in the hands of the states. The weak central government they provided was precisely the type that Americans had been used to prior to the Stamp Act crisis.

After the war, some Americans perceived a need for a stronger central government. Their major concern was the inability of Congress to regulate or protect trade. While part of the British Empire, the colonies had mostly benefited by the trade regulations of Parliament, and colonial merchants had enjoyed the protection of the Royal Navy. Under the articles, however, Congress was prohibited from maintaining a peacetime navy and from regulating either interstate or foreign trade. The result was a chaotic situation for American merchants, artisans, and farmers who produced for the marketplace.

As early as 1783, Americans such as Alexander Hamilton began calling for the creation of a stronger national government. In addition to wanting the national government to be able to protect and regulate trade, they wanted it to be able to tax on its own behalf and to enjoy some control over the actions of the states. In 1787 these Americans were able to convene a meeting in Philadelphia that promptly drew up plans for a strong federal government in the form of the U.S. Constitution.

Although many Americans were happy with the Constitution, many others were unhappy. These Americans, known as anti-federalists, feared that the new government would prove to be just as overbearing as the British government from which they had just fought a war to be free. Much debate would take place in newspapers, pamphlets, and state meetings before their fears would be assuaged.

Virginia Forms a State Government

George Mason et al.

In 1775 the colonial legislatures of Massachusetts and New Hampshire asked Congress to write model constitutions for the soon-to-be-independent states. Congress declined, so these and other states wrote their own. By the time the Declaration of Independence was ratified in 1776, five states—Massachusetts, New Hampshire, South Carolina, New Jersey, and Virginia—had declared their own independence by writing constitutions that negated the power of the king and Parliament.

The Virginia Bill of Rights and Constitution were written by a committee, but most of the work is attributed to George Mason. Adopted less than a month before the Declaration of Independence, which was written mostly by another Virginian, Thomas Jefferson, they reflected the thinking that inspired the Declaration of Independence, the Articles of Confederation, the U.S. Constitution, and the Bill of Rights.

As you read, consider the following questions:
1. How are the Virginia Bill of Rights and Constitution similar to the Declaration of Independence? To the U.S. Constitution?
2. In terms of the powers enjoyed by the executive, legislative, and judicial branches, how and why does the Virginia Constitution differ from the U.S. Constitution?

George Mason et al., *The Constitution of Virginia*, June 29, 1776.

Bill of Rights

A declaration of rights made by the representatives of the good people of Virginia, assembled in full and free convention; which rights do pertain to them and their posterity, as the basis and foundation of government.

SECTION 1. That all men are by nature equally free and independent, and have certain inherent rights, of which, when they enter into a state of society, they cannot, by any compact, deprive or divest their posterity, namely, the enjoyment of life and liberty, with the means of acquiring and possessing property, and pursuing and obtaining happiness and safety.

SEC. 2. That all power is vested in, and consequently derived from, the people; that magistrates are their trustees and servants, and at all times amenable to them.

SEC. 3. That government is, or ought to be, instituted for the common benefit, protection, and security of the people, nation, or community; of all the various modes and forms of government, that is best which is capable of producing the greatest degree of happiness and safety, and is most effectually secured against the danger of maladministration; and that, when any government shall be found inadequate or contrary to these purposes, a majority of the community hath an indubitable, inalienable, and indefeasible right to reform, alter, or abolish it, in such manner as shall be judged most conducive to the public weal.

SEC. 4. That no man, or set of men, are entitled to exclusive or separate emoluments or privileges from the community, but in consideration of public services; which, not being descendible, neither ought the offices of magistrate, legislator, or judge to be hereditary.

SEC. 5. That the legislative and executive powers of the State should be separate and distinct from the judiciary; and that the members of the two first may be restrained from oppression, by feeling and participating the burdens of the people, they should, at fixed periods, be reduced to a private station, return into that body from which they were originally taken, and the vacancies be supplied by frequent, certain, and regular elections, in which all, or any part of the former members, to be again eligible, or ineligible, as the laws shall direct.

SEC. 6. That elections of members to serve as representatives of the people, in assembly, ought to be free; and that all men, having sufficient evidence of permanent common interest with, and attachment to, the community, have the right of suffrage, and cannot be taxed or deprived of their property for public uses, without their own consent, or that of their representatives so elected, nor bound by any law to which they have not, in like manner, assembled, for the public good.

SEC. 7. That all power of suspending laws, or the execution of laws, by any authority, without consent of the representatives of the people, is injurious to their rights, and ought not to be exercised.

SEC. 8. That in all capital or criminal prosecutions a man hath a right to demand the cause and nature of his accusation, to be confronted with the accusers and witnesses, to call for evidence in his favor, and to a speedy trial by an impartial jury of twelve men of his vicinage, without whose unanimous consent he cannot be found guilty; nor can he be compelled to give evidence against himself; that no man be deprived of his liberty, except by the law of the land or the judgment of his peers.

SEC. 9. That excessive bail ought not to be required, nor excessive fines imposed, nor cruel and unusual punishments inflicted.

SEC. 10. That general warrants, whereby an officer or messenger may be commanded to search suspected places without evidence of a fact committed, or to seize any person or persons not named, or whose offence is not particularly described and supported by evidence, are grievous and oppressive, and ought not to be granted.

SEC. 11. That in controversies respecting property, and in suits between man and man, the ancient trial by jury is preferable to any other, and ought to be held sacred.

SEC. 12. That the freedom of the press is one of the great

bulwarks of liberty, and can never be restrained but by despotic governments.

SEC. 13. That a well-regulated militia, composed of the body of the people, trained to arms, is the proper, natural, and safe defence of a free State; that standing armies, in time of peace, should be avoided, as dangerous to liberty; and that in all cases the military should be under strict subordination to, and governed by, the civil power.

SEC. 14. That the people have a right to uniform government; and, therefore, that no government separate from, or independent of the government of Virginia, ought to be erected or established within the limits thereof.

SEC. 15. That no free government, or the blessings of liberty, can be preserved to any people, but by a firm adherence to justice, moderation, temperance, frugality, and virtue, and by frequent recurrence to fundamental principles.

SEC. 16. That religion, or the duty which we owe to our Creator, and the manner of discharging it, can be directed only by reason and conviction, not by force or violence; and therefore all men are equally entitled to the free exercise of religion, according to the dictates of conscience; and that it is the mutual duty of all to practice Christian forbearance, love, and charity towards each other.

The Constitution of Virginia

Whereas George the third, King of Great Britain and Ireland, and elector of Hanover, heretofore intrusted with the exercise of the kingly office in this government, hath endeavoured to prevent, the same into a detestable and insupportable tyranny, by putting his negative on laws the most wholesome and necessary for the public good:

By denying his Governors permission to pass laws of immediate and pressing importance, unless suspended in their operation for his assent, and, when so suspended neglecting to attend to them for many years:

By refusing to pass certain other laws, unless the persons to be benefited by them would relinquish the inestimable right of representation in the legislature:

By dissolving legislative Assemblies repeatedly and continually, for opposing with manly firmness his invasions of the rights of the people:

When dissolved, by refusing to call others for a long space of time, thereby leaving the political system without any legislative head:

By endeavouring to prevent the population of our country, and, for that purpose, obstructing, the laws for the naturalization of foreigners:

By keeping among us, in times of peace, standing armies and ships of war:

By effecting to render the military independent of, and superior to, the civil power:

By combining with others to subject us to a foreign jurisdiction, giving his assent to their pretended acts of legislation:

For quartering large bodies of armed troops among us:

For cutting off our trade with all parts of the world:

For imposing taxes on us without our consent:

For depriving us of the benefits of trial by jury:

For transporting us beyond seas, to be tried for pretended offences:

For suspending our own legislatures, and declaring themselves invested with power to legislate for us in all cases whatsoever:

By plundering our seas, ravaging our coasts, burning our towns, and destroying the lives of our people:

By inciting insurrections of our fellow subjects, with the allurements of forfeiture and confiscation:

By prompting our negroes to rise in arms against us, those very negroes whom, by an inhuman use of his negative, he hath refused us permission to exclude by law:

By endeavouring to bring on the inhabitants of our frontiers the merciless Indian savages, whose known rule of warfare is an undistinguished destruction of all ages, sexes, and conditions of existence:

By transporting, at this time, a large army of foreign mercenaries, to complete the works of death, desolation, and tyranny, already begun with circumstances of cruelty and perfidy unworthy the head of a civilized nation:

By answering our repeated petitions for redress with a repetition of injuries: And finally, by abandoning the helm of government and declaring us out of his allegiance and protection.

By which several acts of misrule, the government of this country, as formerly exercised under the crown of Great Britain, is TOTALLY DISSOLVED.

We therefore, the delegates and representatives of the good people of Virginia, having maturely considered the premises, and viewing with great concern the deplorable conditions to which this once happy country must be reduced, unless some regular, adequate mode of civil polity is speedily adopted, and in compliance with a recommendation of the general Congress, do ordain and declare the future form of government of Virginia to be as followeth:

The legislative, executive, and judiciary department, shall be separate and distinct, so that neither exercise the powers properly belonging to the other: nor shall any person exercise the powers of more than one of them, at the same time; except that the Justices of the County courts shall be eligible to either House of Assembly.

The legislative shall be formed of two distinct branches, who, together, shall be a complete Legislature. They shall meet once, or oftener, every year, and shall be called, The General Assembly of Virginia. One of these shall be called, The House of Delegates, and consist of two Representatives, to be chosen for each county, and for the district of West-Augusta,[1] annually, of such men as actually reside in, and are freeholders of the same, or duly qualified according to law, and also of one Delegate or Representative, to be chosen annually for the city of Williamsburgh, and one for the borough of Norfolk, and a Representative for each of such other cities and boroughs, as may hereafter be allowed particular representation by the legislature; but when any city or borough shall so decrease, as that the

1. all of Virginia west of the Appalachian Mountains

number of persons, having right of suffrage therein, shall have been, for the space of seven Years successively, less than half the number of voters in some one county in Virginia, such city or borough thenceforward shall cease to send a Delegate or Representative to the Assembly.

The other shall be called The Senate, and consist of twenty-four members, of whom thirteen shall constitute a House to proceed on business; for whose election, the different counties shall be divided into twenty-four districts; and each county of the respective district, at the time of the election of its Delegates, shall vote for one Senator, who is actually a resident and freeholder within the district, or duly qualified according to law, and is upwards of twenty-five years of age; and the Sheriffs of each county, within five days at farthest, after the last county election in the district, shall meet at some convenient place, and from the poll, so taken in their respective counties, return, as a Senator, the man who shall have the greatest number of votes in the whole district. To keep up this Assembly by rotation, the districts shall be equally divided into four classes and numbered by lot. At the end of one year after the general election, the six members, elected by the first division, shall be displaced, and the vacancies thereby occasioned supplied from such class or division, by new election, in the manner aforesaid. This rotation shall be applied to each division, according to its number, and continued in due order annually.

The right of suffrage in the election of members for both Houses shall remain as exercised at present; and each House shall choose its own Speaker, appoint its own officers, settle its own rules of proceeding, and direct writs of election, for the supplying intermediate vacancies.

All laws shall originate in the House of Delegates, to be approved of or rejected by the Senate, or to be amended, with consent of the House of Delegates; except money-bills, which in no instance shall be altered by the Senate, but wholly approved or rejected.

A Governor, or chief magistrate, shall be chosen annually by joint ballot of both Houses (to be taken in each House respectively) deposited in the conference room; the boxes examined jointly by a committee of each House, and the numbers severally reported to them, that the appointments may be entered (which shall be the mode of taking the joint ballot of both Houses, in all cases) who shall not continue in that office longer than three years successively, nor be eligible, until the expiration of four years after he shall have been out of that office. An adequate, but moderate salary shall be settled on him, during his continuance in office; and he shall, with the advice of a Council of State, exercise the executive powers of government, according to the laws of this Commonwealth; and shall not, under any presence, exercise any power or prerogative, by virtue of any law, statute or custom of England. But he shall, with the advice of the Council of State, have the power of granting reprieves or pardons, except where the prosecution shall have been carried on by the House of Delegates, or the law shall otherwise particularly direct: in which cases, no reprieve or pardon shall be granted, but by resolve of the House of Delegates.

Either House of the General Assembly may adjourn themselves respectively. The Governor shall not prorogue or adjourn the Assembly, during their sitting, nor dissolve them at any time; but he shall, if necessary, either by advice of the Council of State, or on application of a majority of the House of Delegates, call them before the time to which they shall stand prorogued or adjourned.

A Privy Council, or Council of State, consisting of eight members, shall be chosen, by joint ballot of both Houses of Assembly, either from their own members or the people at large, to assist in the administration of government. They shall annually choose, out of their own members, a President, who, in case of death, inability, or absence of the Governor from the government, shall act as Lieutenant-Governor. Four members shall be sufficient to act, and their advice and proceedings shall be entered on record, and signed by the members present, (to any part whereof, any member may enter his dissent) to be laid before the General Assembly, when called for by them. This Council may appoint their own Clerk, who shall have a salary settled by law, and take an oath of secrecy, in such matters as he shall be directed by the board to conceal. A sum of money, appropriated to that purpose, shall be divided annually among the members in proportion to their attendance; and they shall be incapable, during their continuance in office, of sitting in either House of Assembly. Two members shall be removed, by Joint ballot of both Houses of Assembly, at the end of every three years, and be ineligible for the three next years. These vacancies, as well as those occasioned by death or incapacity, shall be supplied by new elections, in the same manner.

The Delegates for Virginia to the Continental Congress shall be chosen annually, or superseded in the mean time, by joint ballot of both Houses of Assembly.

The present militia officers shall be continued, and vacancies supplied by appointment of the Governor, with the advice of the Privy Council, on recommendations from the respective County Courts; but the Governor and Council shall have a power of suspending any officer, and ordering a Court Martial, on complaint of misbehaviour or inability, or to supply vacancies of officers, happening when in actual service.

The Governor may embody the militia, with the advice of the Privy Council; and when embodied, shall alone have the direction of the militia, under the laws of the country.

The two Houses of Assembly shall, by joint ballot, appoint Judges of the Supreme Court of Appeals, and General Court, Judges in Chancery, Judges of Admiralty, Secretary, and the Attorney-General, to be commissioned by the Governor, and continue in office during good behaviour. In case of death, incapacity, or resignation, the Governor, with the advice of the Privy Council, shall appoint persons to succeed in office, to be approved or displaced by both Houses. These officers shall have fixed and adequate salaries, and, together with all others, holding lucrative offices, and all ministers of the gospel, of every denomination, be incapable of being elected members of either House of Assembly or the Privy Council.

The Governor, with the advice of the Privy Council, shall appoint Justices of the Peace for the counties; and in case of vacancies, or a necessity of increasing the number hereafter, such appointments to be made upon the recommendation of the respective County Courts. The present acting Secretary in Virginia, and Clerks of all the County Courts, shall continue in office. In case of vacancies, either by death, incapacity, or resignation, a Secretary shall be appointed, as before directed; and the Clerks, by the respective Courts. The present and future Clerks shall hold their offices during good behaviour, to be judged of, and determined in the General Court. The Sheriffs and Coroners shall be nominated by the respective Courts, approved by the Governor, with the advice of the Privy Council, and commissioned by the Governor. The Justices shall appoint Constables; and all fees of the aforesaid officers be regulated by law.

The Governor, when he is out of office, and others, offending against the State, either by maladministration, corruption, or other means, by which the safety of the State may be endangered, shall be impeachable by the House of Delegates. Such impeachment to be prosecuted by the Attorney-General, or such other person or persons, as the House may appoint in the General Court, according to the laws of the land. If found guilty, he or they shall be either forever disabled to hold any office under government, or be removed from such office pro tempore, or subjected to such pains or penalties as the laws shall direct.

If all or any of the Judges of the General Court should on good grounds (to be judged of by the House of Delegates) be accused of any of the crimes or offences above mentioned, such House of Delegates may, in like manner, impeach the Judge or Judges so accused, to be prosecuted in the Court of Appeals; and he or they, if found guilty, shall be punished in the same manner as is prescribed in the preceding clause.

Commissions and grants shall run, "In the name of the Commonwealth of Virginia," and bear test by the Governor, with the seal of the Commonwealth annexed. Writs shall run in the same manner, and bear test by the Clerks of the several Courts. Indictments shall conclude, "Against the peace and dignity of the Commonwealth."

A Treasurer shall be appointed annually, by joint ballot of both Houses.

All escheats,[2] penalties, and forfeitures, heretofore going to the King, shall go to the Commonwealth, save only such as the Legislature may abolish, or otherwise provide for.

The territories, contained within the Charters, erecting the Colonies of Maryland, Pennsylvania, North and South Carolina, are hereby ceded, released, and forever confirmed, to the people of these Colonies respectively, with all the rights of property, jurisdiction and government, and all other rights whatsoever, which might, at any time heretofore, have been claimed by Virginia, except the free navigation and use of the rivers Patomaque and Pokomoke,[3] with the property of the Virginia shores and strands, bordering on either of the said rivers, and all improvements, which have been, or shall be made thereon. The western and northern extent of Virginia shall, in all other respects, stand as fixed by the Charter of King James I in the year one thousand six hundred and nine, and by the public treaty of peace between the Courts of Britain and France, in the year one thousand seven hundred and sixty-three; unless by act of this Legislature, one or more governments be established westward of the Alleghany mountains. And no purchases of lands shall be made of the Indian natives, but on behalf of the public, by authority of the General Assembly.

In order to introduce this government, the Representatives of the people met in the convention shall choose a Governor and Privy Council, also such other officers di-

2. property that becomes the state's because the owner died without leaving an heir or any other legal claimants 3. The modern spelling is Potomac and Pocomoke.

rected to be chosen by both Houses as may be judged necessary to be immediately appointed. The Senate to be first chosen by the people to continue until the last day of March next, and the other officers until the end of the succeeding session of Assembly. In case of vacancies, the Speaker of either House shall issue writs for new elections.

The Articles of Confederation

Continental Congress

After ratifying the Declaration of Independence, the Continental Congress appointed a committee to draw up a form of government for the United States. The committee's report was debated and modified extensively before being adopted in 1777. The Articles of Confederation, as the report is known, did not go into effect until 1781, when all thirteen states had ratified them. During the interim, the rules under which the Congress had been operating prevailed.

Several features of the articles are worth mentioning. Article V establishes term limits for congressmen, an issue that has been hotly debated for years. It also retains the old rule that each state, regardless of population or size of delegation, receives one vote in Congress. Article VIII provides that each state's share of the national budget is assessed according to the value of its land and buildings, so that larger states pay more than smaller states. It further stipulates that only the states, and not the Congress, have the authority to levy the taxes by which the state assessments are raised. Article IX implements a convoluted method by which Congress settles claims and suits between and among the various states. In place of a chief executive, this article establishes a thirteen-member "Committee of the States." Article XIII provides that the Articles of Confederation cannot be amended except by unanimous vote of the state legislatures.

As you read, consider the following questions:
1. How are the Articles of Confederation similar to the Vir-

The Articles of Confederation, 1781.

ginia constitution? How are they different? Are the articles mostly similar or mostly different from our present form of government?

2. Why would the Congress propose and the states ratify the form of government created by the Articles of Confederation?

3. Critics of the Articles of Confederation charged that the national government they created was far too weak. Do you agree or disagree? Would the typical American of the day have agreed or disagreed?

Articles of Confederation and Perpetual Union Between the States of New Hampshire, Massachusetts Bay, Rhode Island and Providence Plantations, Connecticut, New York, New Jersey, Pennsylvania, Delaware, Maryland, Virginia, North Carolina, South Carolina and Georgia.

ARTICLE I. The style of this Confederacy shall be "The United States of America."

ARTICLE II. Each state retains its sovereignty, freedom and independence, and every power, jurisdiction and right which is not by this Confederation expressly delegated to the United States in Congress assembled.

ARTICLE III. The said states hereby severally enter into a firm league of friendship with each other for their common defence, the security of their liberties, and their mutual and general welfare, binding themselves to assist each other against all force offered to, or attacks made upon them, or any of them, on account of religion, sovereignty, trade, or any other pretence whatever.

ARTICLE IV. The better to secure and perpetuate mutual friendship and intercourse among the people of the different States in this Union, the free inhabitants of each of these states, paupers, vagabonds and fugitives from justice excepted, shall be entitled to all privileges and immunities of free citizens in the several states; and the people of each state shall have free ingress and regress to and from any other state, and shall enjoy therein all the privileges of trade and commerce, subject to the same duties, impositions and restrictions as the inhabitants thereof respectively; provided, that such restrictions shall not extend so far as to prevent the removal of property imported into any state to any other state of which the owner is an inhabitant; provided also, that no imposition, duties or restriction shall be laid by any state on the property of the United States, or either of them.

If any person guilty of or charged with treason, felony, or other high misdemeanor in any state, shall flee from justice, and be found in any of the United States, he shall upon demand of the governor or executive power of the state from which he fled, be delivered up and removed to the state having jurisdiction of his offense.

Full faith and credit shall be given in each of these states to the records, acts and judicial proceedings of the courts and magistrates of every other state.

ARTICLE V. For the more convenient management of the general interests of the United States, delegates shall be annually appointed in such manner as the legislature of each state shall direct, to meet in Congress on the first Monday in November, in every year, with a power, reserved to each state, to recall its delegates, or any of them, at any time within the year, and to send others in their stead, for the remainder of the year.

No state shall be represented in Congress by less than two, nor by more than seven members; and no person shall be capable of being a delegate for more than three years in any term of six years; nor shall any person, being a delegate, be capable of holding any office under the United States, for which he, or another for his benefit receives any salary, fees or emolument of any kind.

Each state shall maintain its own delegates in a meeting of the states, and while they act as members of the committee of the states.

In determining questions in the United States, in Congress assembled, each state shall have one vote.

Freedom of speech and debate in Congress shall not be

impeached or questioned in any court, or place out of Congress, and the members of Congress shall be protected in their persons from arrests and imprisonments, during the time of their going to and from, and attendance on Congress, except for treason, felony, or breach of the peace.

ARTICLE VI. No state without the consent of the United States in Congress assembled, shall send any embassy to, or receive any embassy from, or enter into any conference, agreement, alliance or treaty with any king, prince or state; nor shall any person holding any office of profit or trust under the United States, or any of them, accept of any present, emolument, office or title of any kind whatever from any king, prince or foreign state; nor shall the United States in Congress assembled, or any of them, grant any title of nobility.

No two or more states shall enter into any treaty, confederation or alliance whatever between them without the consent of the United States in Congress assembled, specifying accurately the purposes for which the same is to be entered into, and how long it shall continue.

No state shall lay any impost or duties, which may interfere with any stipulations in treaties, entered into by the United States in Congress assembled, with any king, prince or state, in pursuance of any treaties already proposed by Congress to the courts of France and Spain.

No vessels of war shall be kept up in time of peace by any state, except such number only as shall be deemed necessary by the United States in Congress assembled, for the defence of such state, or its trade; nor shall any body of forces be kept up by any state, in time of peace except such number only, as in the judgment of the United States in Congress assembled, shall be deemed requisite to garrison the forts necessary for the defence of such state; but every state shall always keep up a well regulated and disciplined militia, sufficiently armed and accoutered, and shall provide and constantly have ready for use, in public stores, a due number of field pieces and tents, and a proper quantity of arms, ammunition and camp equipage.

No state shall engage in any war without the consent of the United States in Congress assembled, unless such state be actually invaded by enemies, or shall have received certain advice of a resolution being formed by some nation of Indians to invade such state, and the danger is so imminent as not to admit of a delay, till the United States in Congress assembled can be consulted: nor shall any state grant commissions to any ships or vessels of war, nor letters of marque or reprisal,[1] except it be after a declaration of war by the United States in Congress assembled, and then only against the kingdom or state and the subjects thereof, against which war has been so declared, and under such regulations as shall be established by the United States in Congress assembled, unless such state be infested by pirates, in which case vessels of war be fitted out for that occasion, and kept so long as the danger shall continue, or until the United States in Congress assembled shall determine otherwise.

ARTICLE VII. When land forces are raised by any state for the common defence, all officers of or under the rank of colonel, shall be appointed by the Legislature of each state respectively by whom such forces shall be raised, or in such manner as such state shall direct, and all vacancies shall be filled up by the state which first made the appointment.

ARTICLE VIII. All charges of war, and all other expenses that shall be incurred for the common defence or general welfare, and allowed by the United States in Congress assembled, shall be defrayed out of a common treasury, which shall be supplied by the several states, in proportion to the value of all land within each state, granted to or surveyed for any person, as such land and the buildings and improvements thereon shall be estimated according to such mode as the United States in Congress assembled, shall from time to time direct and appoint.

The taxes for paying that proportion shall be laid and

1. Letters of marque and reprisal were legal documents that authorized privately owned armed vessels, known as privateers, to prey on the shipping of a specific enemy.

levied by the authority and direction of the legislatures of the several states within the time agreed upon by the United States in Congress assembled.

ARTICLE IX. The United States in Congress assembled, shall have the sole and exclusive right and power of determining on peace and war except in the cases mentioned in the sixth article; of sending and receiving ambassadors; entering into treaties and alliances; provided that no treaty of commerce shall be made whereby the legislative power of the respective states shall be restrained from imposing such imposts and duties on foreigners, as their own people are subjected to, or from prohibiting the exportation or importation of any species of goods or commodities whatsoever; of establishing rules for deciding in all cases, what captures on land or water shall be legal, and in what manner prizes taken by land or naval forces in the service of the United States shall be divided or appropriated; of granting letters of marque and reprisal in times of peace; appointing courts for the trial of piracies and felonies committed on the high seas and establishing courts for receiving and determining finally appeals in all cases of captures, provided that no member of Congress shall be appointed a judge of any of said courts.

The United States in Congress assembled shall also be the last resort on appeal in all disputes and differences now subsisting or that hereafter may arise between two or more states concerning boundary, jurisdiction or any other cause whatever; which authority shall always be exercised in the manner following. Whenever the legislative or executive authority or lawful agent of any state in controversy with another shall present a petition to Congress, stating the matter in question and praying for a hearing, notice thereof shall be given by order of Congress to the legislative or executive authority of the other state in controversy, and a day assigned for the appearance of the parties by their lawful agents, who shall then be directed to appoint by joint consent commissioners or judges to constitute a court for hearing and determining the matter in question:

but if they can not agree, Congress shall name three persons out of each of the United States, and from the list of such persons each party shall alternately strike out one, the petitioners beginning, until the number shall be reduced to thirteen; and from that number not less than seven, nor more than nine names, as Congress shall direct, shall in the presence of Congress be drawn out by lot, and the persons whose names shall be so drawn or any five of them, shall be commissioners or judges, to hear and finally determine the controversy, so always as a major part of the judges who shall hear the cause shall agree in the determination: and if either party shall neglect to attend at the day appointed, without showing reasons, which Congress judge sufficient, or being present shall refuse to strike, the Congress shall proceed to nominate three persons out of each state, and the Secretary of Congress shall strike in behalf of such party absent or refusing; and the judgment and sentence of the court to be appointed, in the manner before prescribed, shall be final and conclusive; and if any of the parties shall refuse to submit to the authority of such court, or to appear or defend their claim or cause, the court shall nevertheless proceed to pronounce sentence, or judgment, which shall in like manner be final and decisive, the judgment or sentence and other proceeds being in either case transmitted to Congress, and lodged among the acts of Congress for the security of the parties concerned: provided that every commissioner, before he sits in judgment, shall take an oath to be administered by one of the judges of the supreme or superior court of the state where the cause shall be tried, "well and truly to hear and determine the matter in question, according to the best of his judgment without favor, affection, or hope of reward": provided also that no state shall be deprived of territory for the benefit of the United States.

All controversies concerning the private right of soil claimed under different grants of two or more states, whose jurisdiction as they may respect such lands, and the states which passed such grants are adjusted, the said grants or either of them being at the same time claimed to have originated antecedent to such settlement of jurisdiction, shall on the petition of either party to the Congress of the United States, be finally determined as near as may be in the same manner as is before prescribed for deciding disputes respecting territorial jurisdiction between the different states.

The United States in Congress assembled shall also have the sole and exclusive right and power of regulating the alloy and value of coin struck by their own authority, or by that of the respective states, fixing the standard of weights and measures throughout the United States, regulating the trade, and managing all affairs with the Indians, not members of any of the states, provided that the legislative right of any state within its own limits be not infringed or violated; establishing and regulating post offices from one state to another, throughout all the United States, and exacting such postage on the papers passing through the same as may be requisite to defray the expenses of the said office; appointing all officers of the land forces, in the service of the United States, excepting regimental officers; appointing all the officers of the naval forces, and commissioning all officers whatever in the service of the United States; making rules for the government and regulation of said land and naval forces, and directing their operations.

The United States in Congress assembled shall have authority to appoint a committee, to sit in the recess of Congress, to be denominated "a Committee of the States," and to consist of one delegate from each state; and to appoint such other committees and civil officers as may be necessary for managing the general affairs of the United States under their direction; to appoint one of their number to preside, provided that no person be allowed to serve in the office of president more than one year in any term of three years; to ascertain the necessary sums of money to be raised for the service of the United States, and to appropriate and apply the same for defraying the public expenses; to borrow money, or emit bills on the credit of the United States, transmitting every half year to the respective states an account of the sums of money so borrowed or emitted; to build and equip a navy; to agree upon the number of land forces, and to make requisitions from each state for its quota, in proportion to the number of white inhabitants in such state; which requisition shall be binding, and thereupon the legislature of each state shall appoint the regimental officers, raise the men and clothe, arm and equip them in a soldierlike manner, at the expense of the United States; and the officers and men so clothed, armed and equipped shall march to the place appointed, and within the time agreed on by the United States in Congress assembled: but if the United States in Congress assembled shall, on consideration of circumstances judge proper that any state should not raise men or should raise a smaller number than its quota, and that any other state should raise a greater number of men than the quota thereof, such extra number shall be raised, officered, clothed, armed and equipped in the same manner as the quota of such state, unless the legislature of such state shall judge that such extra number can not be safely spared out of the same, in which case they shall raise, officer, clothe, arm and equip as many of such extra number as they judge can be safely spared. And the officers and men so clothed, armed and equipped, shall march to the place appointed, and within the time agreed on by the United States in Congress assembled.

The United States in Congress assembled shall never engage in war, nor grant letters of marque and reprisal in time of peace, nor enter into any treaties or alliances, nor coin money, nor regulate the value thereof, nor ascertain the sums and expenses necessary for the defence and welfare of the United States, or any of them, nor emit bills, nor borrow money on the credit of the United States, nor appropriate money, nor agree upon the number of vessels of war, to be built or purchased, or the number of land or sea forces to be raised, nor appoint a commander-in-chief of the army or navy, unless nine states assent to the same: nor shall a question on any other point, except for adjourning from day to day be determined, unless by the votes of a majority of the United States in Congress assembled.

The Congress of the United States shall have power to adjourn to any time within the year, and to any place within the United States, so that no period of adjournment be for a longer duration than the space of six months; and shall publish the journal of their proceedings monthly, except such parts thereof relating to treaties, alliances or military operations, as in their judgment require secrecy; and the yeas and nays of the delegates of each state on any question shall be entered on the journal, when it is desired by any delegate; and the delegates of a state, or any of them, at his or their request, shall be furnished with transcript of the said journal, except such parts as are above excepted to lay before the legislatures of the several states.

ARTICLE X. The Committee of the States, or any nine of them shall be authorized to execute, in the recess of Congress, such of the powers of Congress as the United States in Congress assembled by the consent of nine states, shall from time to time think expedient to vest them with; provided that no power be delegated to the said committee for the exercise of which, by the Articles of Confederation, the voice of nine states in the Congress of the United States assembled is requisite.

ARTICLE XI. Canada acceding to this Confederation, and joining in the measures of the United States, shall be admitted into, and entitled to all the advantages of this Union: but no other colony shall be admitted into the same, unless such admission be agreed to by nine states.

ARTICLE XII. All bills of credit emitted, moneys borrowed and debts contracted by, or under the authority of Congress, before the assembling of the United States, in pursuance of the present Confederation, shall be deemed and considered as a charge against the United States, for payment and satisfaction whereof the said United States and the public faith are hereby solemnly pledged.

ARTICLE XIII. Every state shall abide by the determinations of the United States in Congress assembled, on all questions which by this Confederation are submitted to them. And the Articles of this Confederation shall be inviolably observed by every state, and the Union shall be perpetual; nor shall any alteration at any time hereafter be made in any of them, unless such alteration be agreed in a Congress of the United States, and be afterwards confirmed by the legislatures of every state.

James Madison Argues for a Stronger National Government

James Madison

Merchants were among the loudest of those who complained that the Articles of Confederation were too weak. Their biggest complaint was with Article 9, which prohibited Congress from making commercial treaties with America's various trading partners. The individual states retained this power themselves, and yet none of them were large enough to extract favorable trade concessions from any European nation. Meanwhile, all trading advantages that American merchants had enjoyed under the protection of the British Empire had been lost. As a result, many merchants were demanding that the Articles of Confederation be amended so as to protect America's commercial interests.

James Madison was a former congressman from Virginia and a future president. This selection is taken from a 1785 letter to his friend, James Monroe, also a future president. In it, Madison argues that Article 9 should be amended to give Congress the power to regulate international trade. He further argues that other weaknesses in the articles should be amended before the allegiance to the United States of other powerful interest groups is undermined.

As you read, consider the following questions:
1. To Madison, what is the greatest weakness of the Articles of Confederation in general?

James Madison, *Letter to James Monroe*, August 7, 1785.

2. Why did Madison, a southern planter, want to improve the economic situation for merchants, most of whom lived in the northern states?

Viewing in the abstract the question whether the power of regulating trade, to a certain degree at least, ought to be vested in Congress, it appears to me not to admit of a doubt, but that it should be decided in the affirmative. If it be necessary to regulate trade at all, it surely is necessary to lodge the power, where trade can be regulated with effect, and experience has confirmed what reason foresaw, that it can never be so regulated by the States acting in their separate capacities. They can no more exercise this power separately, than they could separately carry on war, or separately form treaties of alliance or Commerce. The nature of the thing therefore proves the former power, no less than the latter, to be within the reason of the federal Constitution. Much indeed is it to be wished, as I conceive, that no regulations of trade, that is to say, no restrictions or imposts whatever, were necessary. A perfect freedom is the System which would be my choice. But before such a system will be eligible perhaps for the U.S. they must be out of debt; before it will be attainable, all other nations must concur in it. Whilst any one of these imposes on our Vessels seamen &c[1] in their ports, clogs from which they exempt their own, we must either retort the distinction, or renounce not merely a just profit, but our only defence against the danger which may most easily beset us. Are we not at this moment under this very alternative? The policy of G.B.[2] (to say nothing of other nations) has shut against us the channels without which our trade with her must be a losing one; and she has consequently the triumph, as we have the chagrin, of seeing accomplished her prophetic threats, that our independence, should forfeit commercial advantages for which it would not recompence us with any new channels of trade. What is

1. etc.   2. Great Britain

to be done? Must we remain passive victims to foreign politics; or shall we exert the lawful means which our independence has put into our hands, of extorting redress? The very question would be an affront to every Citizen who loves his Country. What then are those means? Retaliating regulations of trade only. How are these to be effectuated? only by harmony in the measures of the States. How is this harmony to be obtained? only by an acquiescence of all the States in the opinion of a reasonable majority. If Congress as they are now constituted, can not be trusted with the power of digesting and enforcing this opinion, let them be otherwise constituted: let their numbers be encreased, let them be chosen oftener, and let their period of service be short[e]ned; or if any better medium than Congress can be proposed, by which the wills of the States may be concentered, let it be substituted; or lastly let no regulation of trade adopted by Congress be in force untill it shall have been ratified by a certain proportion of the States. But let us not sacrifice the end to the means: let us not rush on certain ruin in order to avoid a possible danger. I conceive it to be of great importance that the defects of the federal system should be amended, not only because such amendments will make it better answer the purpose for which it was instituted, but because I apprehend danger to its very existence from a continuance of defects which expose a part if not the whole of the empire to severe distress. The suffering part, even when the minor part, can not long respect a Government which is too feeble to protect their interest; But when the suffering part come to be the major part, and they despair of seeing a protecting energy given to the General Government, from what motives is their allegiance to be any longer expected. Should G.B. persist in the machinations which distress us; and seven or eight of the States be hindered by the others from obtaining relief by federal means, I own, I tremble at the anti-federal expedients into which the former may be tempted. As to the objection against intrusting Congress with a power over trade, drawn from the diversity of interests in the States, it may be answered. 1. that if this objection had been listened to, no confederation could have ever taken place among the States. 2. that if it ought now to be listened to, the power held by Congress of forming Commercial treaties by which 9 States may indirectly dispose of the Commerce of the residue, ought to be immediately revoked. 3. that the fact is that a case can scarcely be imagined in which it would be the interest of any 2/3ds of the States to oppress the remaining 1/3d. 4. that the true question is whether the commercial interests of the States do not meet in more points than they differ. To me it is clear that they do: and if they do there are so many more reasons for, than against, submitting the commercial interest of each State to the direction and care of the Majority. Put the West India trade alone, in which the interest of every State is involved, into the scale against all the inequalities which may result from any probable regulation by nine States, and who will say that the latter ought to preponderate? I have heard the different interest which the Eastern States[3] have as Carriers pointed out as a ground of caution to the Southern States who have no bottoms[4] of their own agst[5] their concurring hastily in retaliations on G.B. But will the present system of G.B. ever give the Southern States bottoms: and if they are not their own Carriers I shod.[6] suppose it no mark either of folly or incivility to give our custom to our brethren rather than to those who have not yet entitled themselves to the name of friends.

In detailing these sentiments I have nothing more in view than to prov[e] the readiness with which I obey your requests. As far as they are just they must have been often suggested in the discussions of Congress on the subject. I can not even give them weight by saying that I have reason to believe they would be relished in the public Councils of this State. From the trials of which I have been a witness I augur that great difficulties will be encountered in every attempt to prevail on the Legislature[7] to part with power. The

3. New England 4. oceangoing vessels 5. against 6. should 7. not Congress, but the Virginia state legislature

thing itself is not only unpalatable, but the arguments which plead for it have not their full force on minds unaccustomed to consider the interests of the State as they are interwoven with those of the Confederacy much less as they may be affected by foreign politics whilst those wch.[8] plead agst. it, are not only specious, but in their nature popular: and for that reason, sure of finding patrons. Add to all this that the mercantile interest which has taken the lead in rousing the public attention of other States, is in this so exclusively occupied in British Commerce that what little weight they have will be most likely to fall into the opposite scale. The only circumstance which promises a favorable hearing to the meditated proposition of Congs.[9] is that the power which it asks is to be exerted agst. G.B., and the proposition will consequently be seconded by the animosities which still prevail in a strong degree agst. her.

8. which   9. Congress

A Virginian Argues Against a Stronger National Government

A Federal Republican

While James Madison argued for a strong national government of the type created by the U.S. Constitution, many of his fellow Virginians were appalled by the specter of such a government. To their minds, the American Revolution had been fought to remove exactly such a government from a position of dominance over the colonial assemblies. The U.S. Constitution was the last thing they wanted because they believed it would implement an oppressive national government that the individual states would be hard-pressed to resist.

A Federal Republican was an anonymous Virginian who was opposed to ratifying the U.S. Constitution. In this selection from a letter he wrote to a newspaper editor, he argues that the Constitution places entirely too much power in the hands of the federal government. In particular, he opposes giving the federal government the power to raise its own troops, which he believes will be used to suppress any opposition to the federal government.

As you read, consider the following questions:
1. Why does A Federal Republican fear federal troops? Do his fears seem reasonable? If so, why? If not, why not?
2. How does A Federal Republican categorize the Constitutional Convention and the founders? How does this description fit with other descriptions you have heard or read about?

A Federal Republican, "Letter to the Editor," *The Norfolk and Portsmouth Register*, March 5, 1788.

By the Articles of Confederation, the congress of the United States was vested with powers for conducting the common concerns of the continent. They had the sole and exclusive right and power of determining on peace and war; of sending and receiving ambassadors; of entering into treaties and alliances; and of pointing out the respective quotas of men and money which each state should furnish. But it was expressly provided that the money to be supplied by each state should be raised by the authority and direction of the legislature thereof—thus reserving to the states the important privilege of levying taxes upon their citizens in such manner as might be most conformable to their peculiar circumstances and form of government. With powers thus constituted was congress enabled to unite the general exertions of the continent in the cause of liberty and to carry us triumphantly through a long and bloody war. It was not until sometime after peace and a glorious independence had been established that defects were discovered in that system of federal government which had procured to us those blessings. It was then perceived that the Articles of Confederation were inadequate to the purposes of the union; and it was particularly suggested as necessary to vest in congress the further power of exclusively regulating the commerce of the United States, as well to enable us, by a system more uniform, to counteract the policy of foreign nations, as for other important reasons. Upon this principle, a general convention of the United States was proposed to be held, and deputies were accordingly appointed by twelve of the states[1] charged with power to revise, alter, and amend the Articles of Confederation. When these deputies met, instead of confining themselves to the powers with which they were entrusted, they pronounced all amendments to the Articles of Confederation wholly impracticable; and with a spirit of amity and concession truly remarkable proceeded to form a government entirely new,

1. Rhode Island did not send delegates to the Constitutional Convention.

and totally different in its principles and its organization. Instead of a congress whose members could serve but three years out of six—and then to return to a level with their fellow citizens; and who were liable at all times, whenever the states might deem it necessary, to be recalled—congress, by this new constitution, will be composed of a body whose members during the time they are appointed to serve, can receive no check from their constituents. Instead of the powers formerly granted to congress of ascertaining each state's quota of men and money—to be raised by the legislatures of the different states in such a mode as they might think proper—congress, by this new government, will be invested with the formidable powers of raising armies, and lending money, totally independent of the different states. They will moreover, have the power of leading troops among you in order to suppress those struggles which may sometimes happen among a free people, and which tyranny will impiously brand with the name of sedition. On one day the state collector will call on you for your proportion of those taxes which have been laid on you by the general assembly, where you are fully and adequately represented; on the next will come the Continental collector to demand from you those taxes which shall be levied by the continental congress, where the whole state of Virginia will be represented by only ten men! Thus shall we imprudently confer on so small a number the very important power of taking our money out of our pockets, and of levying taxes without control—a right which the wisdom of our state constitution will, in vain, have confided to the most numerous branch of the legislature. Should the sheriff or state collector in any manner aggrieve you either in person or property, these sacred rights are amply secured by the most solemn compact. Beside, the arm of government is always at hand to shield you from his injustice and oppression. But if a Continental collector, in the execution of his office, should invade your freedom (according to this new government, which has expressly declared itself paramount to all state laws and constitutions) the state of which you are a citizen will have no authority to afford you relief. A continental court may, indeed, be established in the state, and it may be urged that you will find a remedy here; but, my fellow citizens, let me ask, what protection this will afford you against the insults or rapacity of a continental officer, when he will have it in his power to appeal to the seat of congress perhaps at several hundred miles distance, and by this means oblige you to expend hundreds of pounds in obtaining redress for twenty shillings unjustly extorted? Thus will you be necessarily compelled either to make a bold effort to extricate yourselves from these grievous and oppressive extortions, or you will be fatigued by fruitless attempts into the quiet and peaceable surrender of those rights, for which the blood of your fellow citizens has been shed in vain. But the latter will, no doubt, be the melancholy fate of a people once inspired with the love of liberty, as the power vested in congress of sending troops for suppressing insurrections will always enable them to stifle the first struggles of freedom.

—A Federal Republican

Alexander Hamilton Argues for a Stronger National Government

Alexander Hamilton

Ratified in 1781, the Articles of Confederation gave the patriots exactly the kind of decentralized national government they wanted. With a weak executive branch and a virtually nonexistent judicial branch, all power was concentrated in Congress, which did not have the power to control the various states. Under the articles, the state legislatures were the supreme authorities within their own boundaries, and they were not challenged by a stronger authority, such as they had been by Parliament.

Almost immediately after their ratification, however, certain individuals began to find fault with the kind of national government created by the articles. Alexander Hamilton, future Secretary of the Treasury, represented New York in Congress for a year. Appalled by Congress's inability to do what he wanted it to do, in 1783 he drew up this proposal calling for a constitutional convention by which the articles could be strengthened. It was never submitted to Congress for consideration, however, because the several congressmen to whom he showed it were not very supportive. Ironically, many of its proposals were later implemented into the U.S. Constitution.

As you read, consider the following questions:
1. What does Hamilton consider to be the major shortcoming of the Articles of Confederation? What does he consider to be its major strength?

Alexander Hamilton, *Resolution Intended to Be Submitted to Congress at Princeton in 1783; but Abandoned for Want of Support*, June 20, 1783.

2. Why do you suppose Congress refused to discuss Hamilton's proposal?

―――――――――――――――――――――――――――――

Whereas in the opinion of this Congress the confederation of the United States is defective in the following essential points, to wit:

First and generally in confining the power of the federal government within too narrow limits, withholding from it that efficacious authority and influence in all matters of general concern which are indispensable to the harmony and welfare of the whole—embarrassing general provisions by unnecessary details and inconvenient exceptions incompatible with their nature tending only to create jealousies and disputes respecting the proper bounds of the authority of the United States and of that of the particular states, and a mutual interference of the one with the other.

Secondly. In confounding legislative and executive powers in a single body, as that of determining on the number and quantity of force, land and naval, to be employed for the common defence, and of directing their operations when raised and equipped with that of ascertaining and making requisitions for the necessary sums or quantities of money to be paid by the respective states into the common treasury; contrary to the most approved and well founded maxims of free government which require that the legislative executive and judicial authorities should be deposited in distinct and separate hands.

Thirdly. In the want of a Federal Judicature having cognizance of all matters of general concern in the last resort, especially those in which foreign nations, and their subjects are interested; from which defect, by the interference of the local regulations of particular states militating directly or indirectly against the powers vested in the Union, the national treaties will be liable to be infringed, the national faith to be violated and the public tranquillity to be disturbed.

Fourthly. In vesting the United States in Congress assembled with the *power of general taxation*, comprehended in that of "ascertaining the necessary sums of money to be raised for the common defence and of appropriating and applying the same for defraying the public expences"—and yet rendering that power, so essential to the existence of the union, nugatory, by witholding from them all controul over either the imposition or the collection of the taxes for raising the sums required; whence it happens that the inclinations not the abilities of the respective states are in fact the criterion of their contributions to the common expence; and the public burthen has fallen and will continue to fall with very unequal weight.

5thly. In fixing a rule for determining the proportion of each state towards the common expence which if practicable at all, must in the execution be attended with great expence inequality uncertainty and difficulty.

6thly. In authorising Congress "to borrow money or emit bills on the credit of the United States" without the power of establishing funds to secure the repayment of the money borrowed or the redemption of the bills emitted; from which must result one of these evils, either a want of sufficient credit in the first instance to borrow, or to circulate the bills emitted, whereby in great national exigencies the public safety may be endangered, or in the second instance, frequent infractions of the public engagements, disappointments to lenders, repetitions of the calamities of depreciating paper, a continuance of the injustice and mischiefs of an unfunded debt, and first or last the annihilation of public credit. Indeed, in authorising Congress at all to emit an *unfunded* paper as the sign of value, a resource which though useful in the infancy, of this country, indispensable in the commencement of the revolution, ought not to continue a formal part of the constit[u]tion, nor ever hereafter to be employed, being in its nature pregnant with abuses and liable to be made the engine of imposition and fraud, holding out temptations equally pernicious to the integrity of government and to the morals of the people.

7thly. In not making proper or competent provision for interior or exterior defence: for interior defence, by leaving it to the individual states to appoint all regimental officers of the land forces, to raise the men in their own way, to cloath arm and equip them at the expence of the United States; from which circumstances have resulted and will hereafter result, great confusion in the military department, continual disputes of rank, languid and disproportionate levies of men, an enormous increase of expence for want of system and uniformity in the manner of conducting them, and from the competitions of state bounties; by an ambiguity in the 4th clause of the 6th article, susceptible of a construction which would devolve upon the particular states in time of peace the care of their own defence both by sea and land and would preclude the United States from raising a single regiment or building a single ship, before a declaration of war, or an actual commencement of hostilities; a principle dangerous to the confederacy in different respects, by leaving the United States at all times unprepared for the defence of their common rights, obliging them to begin to raise an army and to build and equip a navy at the moment they would have occasion to employ them, and by putting into the hands of a few states, who from their local situations are more immediately exposed, all the standing forces of the country; thereby not only leaving the care of the safety of the whole to a part which will naturally be both unwilling and unable to make effectual provision at its particular expence, but also furnishing grounds of jealousy and distrust between the states; unjust in its operation to those states, in whose hands they are by throwing the exclusive burthen of maintaining those forces upon them, while their neighbours immediately and all the states ultimately would share the benefits of their services: For exterior defence, in authorising Congress "to build and equip a navy" without providing any means of manning it, either by requisitions of the states, by the power of registering and drafting the seamen in rotation, or by embargoes in cases of emergency to induce them to accept employment on board the ships of war; the omission of all which leaves no other resource than voluntary inlistment, a resource which has been found ineffectual in every country, and for reasons of peculiar force in this.

8thly. In not vesting in the United States a general superintendence of trade, equally necessary in the view of revenue and regulation; of revenue because duties on commerce, when moderate, are one of the most agreeable and productive species of it, which cannot without great disadvantages be imposed by particular states, while others refrain from doing it, but must be imposed in concert, and by laws operating upon the same principles, at the same moment, in all the states, otherwise those states which should not impose them would engross the commerce of such of their neighbours as did; of regulation because by general prohibitions of particular articles, by a judicious arrangement of duties, sometimes by bounties on the manufacture or exportation of certain commodities, injurious branches of commerce might be discouraged, favourable branches encouraged, useful products and manufactures promoted; none of which advantages can be as effectually attained by separate regulations, without a general superintending power; because also, it is essential to the due observance of the commercial stipulations of the United States with foreigner powers, an in[ter]ference with which will be unavoidable if the different states have the exclusive regulation of their own trade and of course the construction of the treaties entered into.

9thly. In defeating essential powers by provisos and limitations inconsistent with their nature; as the power of making treaties with foreign nations, "provided that no treaty of commerce shall be made whereby the legislative power of the respective states shall be restrained from imposing such imposts and duties on foreigners as their own people are subjected to, or from prohibitting the importation or exportation of any species of goods or commodities whatsoever," a proviso susceptible of an interpretation which includes a constitutional possibility of defeating the treaties of commerce entered into by the United States: As also the power "of regulating the trade and managing all affairs with the Indians not members of any of the states *provided* that the legislative right of any state within its own limits be not infringed or violated"—and others of a similar nature.

10thly. In granting the United States the sole power "of regulating the alloy and value of coin struck by their own authority, or by that of the respective states" without the power of regulating the foreign coin in circulation; though the one is essential to the due exercise of the other, as there ought to be such proportions maintained between the na-

Alexander Hamilton urged Congress to strengthen the national government. Many of his ideas were later incorporated into the U.S. Constitution.

tional and foreign coin as will give the former a preference in all internal negotiations; and without the latter power, the operations of government in a matter of primary importance to the commerce and finances of the United States will be exposed to numberless obstructions.

11thly. In requiring the assent of *nine* states to matters of principal importance and of seven to all others, except adjournments from day to day; a rule destructive of vigour, consistency or expedition in the administration of affairs, tending to subject the *sense* of the majority to *that* of the minority, by putting it in the power of a small combination to retard and even to frustrate the most necessary measures and to oblige the greater number, in cases which require speedy determinations, as happens in the most interesting concerns of the community, to come into the views of the smaller, the evils of which have been felt in critical conjunctures and must always make the spirit of government, a spirit of compromise and expedient rather than of system and energy.

12thly. In vesting in the Federal government the sole direction of the interests of the United States in their intercourse with foreign nations, without empowering it to pass all general laws in aid and support of the laws of nations; for the want of which authority, the faith of the United States may be broken, their reputation sullied, and their peace interrupted by the negligence or misconception of any particular state.

And Whereas experience hath clearly manifested that the powers reserved to the Union in the Confederation are unequal to the purpose of effectually d[r]awing forth the resources of the respective members for the common welfare and defence; whereby the United States have upon several occasions been exposed to the most critical and alarming situations; have wanted an army adequate to their defence and proportioned to the abilities of the country—have on account of that deficiency seen essential posts reduced, others eminently endangered, whole states and large parts of others overrun and ravaged by small bodies of the enemy's forces—have been destitute of sufficient means of feeding, cloathing, paying and appointing that army, by which the troops, rendered less efficient for military operations, have been exposed to sufferings, which nothing but unparallelled patience perseverance and patriotism could have endured—whereby also the United States have been too often compelled to make the administration of their affairs a succession of temporary expedients, inconsistent with order economy energy or a scrupulous adherence to the public engagements; and now find themselves at the close of a glorious struggle for independence, without any certain means of doing justice to those who have been its principal supporters—to an army which has bravely fought and patiently suffered—to citizens who have chearfully lent their money, and to others who have in different ways contributed their property and their personal service to the common cause; obliged to rely for the only effectual mode of doing that justice, by funding the debt on solid securities, on the precarious concurrence of thirteen destinct deliberations, the dissent of either of which may defeat the plan and leave these states at this early period of their existence involved in all the disgrace and mischiefs of violated faith and national bankruptcy.

And Whereas notwithstanding we have by the blessing of providence so far happily escaped the complicated dangers of such a situation, and now see the object of our wishes secured by an honorable peace, it would be unwise to hazard a repetition of the same dangers and embarrassments in any future war in which these states may be engaged, or to continue this extensive empire under a government unequal to its protection and prosperity.

And Whereas it is essential to the happiness and security of these states, that their union, should be established on the most solid foundations, and it is manifest that this desireable object cannot be effected but by a government capable both in peace and war of making every member of the Union contribute in just proportion to the common necessities, and of combining and directing the forces and wills of the several parts to a general end; to which purposes in the opinion of Congress the present confederation is altogether inadequate.

And Whereas on the spirit which may direct the councils and measures of these states at the present juncture may depend their future safety and welfare; Congress conceive it to be their duty freely to state to their constituents the defects which by experience have been discovered in the present plan of the Federal Union and solemnly to call their attention to a revisal and amendment of the same:

Therefore Resolved that it be earnestly recommended to the several states to appoint a convention to meet at ___ on the ___ day of ___ with full powers to revise the confederation and to adopt and propose such alterations as to them shall appear necessary to be finally approved or rejected by the states respectively—and that a Committee of ___ be appointed to prepare an address upon the subject.

A South Carolinian Argues Against a Stronger National Government

Rawlins Lowndes

When the Constitutional Convention submitted the U.S. Constitution to the various states for ratification in 1787, it sparked many lively debates in the state legislatures. While many leaders spoke in favor of the strong national government that the Constitution would implement, many others expressed their fears that national government under the Constitution would be just as oppressive as parliamentary rule had been before the Revolution. Oftentimes, these leaders praised the Articles of Confederation for establishing exactly the type of national government that the patriots had demanded during the struggle with Great Britain.

Rawlins Lowndes was a longtime member of the South Carolina colonial and state assemblies, and in 1778–1779 he served as the state's chief executive. When the U.S. Constitution was debated before the South Carolina state legislature in 1788, he was the most prominent figure to speak against its ratification. This selection is an excerpt from a transcription of a speech he gave before the legislature during the debate.

As you read, consider the following questions:
1. Why did Lowndes think more highly of the Articles of Confederation than he did of the U.S. Constitution?
2. What did Lowndes fear would happen if the Constitution was ratified?

Rawlins Lowndes, speech before the South Carolina State Legislature, 1788.

Hon. Rawlins Lowndes declared himself almost willing to give up his post,[1] finding he was opposed by such a phalanx of able antagonists, any one of them possessing sufficient abilities to contend with him; but as a number of respectable members, men of good sense, though not in the habit of speaking in public, had requested that he would state his sentiments, for the purpose of gaining information on such points as seemed to require it,—rather in compliance, therefore, with their wishes, than any inclination on his part, he should make a few further observations on the subject. Much had been said, from different parts of the house, against the old Confederation—that it was such a futile, inefficient, impolitic government as to render us the objects of ridicule and contempt in the eyes of other nations. He could not agree to this, because there did not appear any evidence of the fact, and because the names of those gentlemen who had signed the old Confederation were eminent for patriotism, virtue, and wisdom,—as much so as any set of men that could be found in America,—and their prudence and wisdom particularly appeared in the care which they had taken sacredly to guaranty the sovereignty of each state. The treaty of peace expressly agreed to acknowledge us as free, sovereign, and independent states, which privileges we lived at present in the exercise of. But this new Constitution at once swept those privileges away, being sovereign over all; so that this state would dwindle into a mere skeleton of what it was; its legislative powers would be pared down to little more than those now vested in the corporation; and he should value the honor of a seat in the legislature in no higher estimation than a seat in the city council. Adverting to the powers given to the President, he considered them as enormous, particularly in being allowed to interfere in the election of members in the House of Representatives; astonishing that we had not this reserved to us, when the senators were to

1. He was a state legislator.

be chosen from that body:—thinks it might be so managed that the different legislatures should be limited to the passing a few laws for regulating ferries and roads.

The honorable gentleman went into an investigation of the weight of our representation in the proposed government, which he thought would be merely virtual, similar to what we were allowed in England, whilst under the British government. We were then told that we were represented in Parliament; and this would, in the event, prove just such another. The mode of choosing senators was exceedingly exceptionable. It had been the practice formerly to choose the Senate or council for this state from that house, which practice proved so inconvenient and oppressive, that, when we framed our present Constitution, great care was taken to vest the power of electing the Senate originally with the people, as the best plan for securing their rights and privileges. He wished to know in what manner it was proposed to elect the five representatives. Was it to be done in this city? or would some districts return one member, and others none at all?

Still greater difficulties would be found in the choice of a President, because he must have a majority of ninety-one votes in his favor. For the first President there was one man to whom all America looked up, (General Washington,) and for whom he most heartily would vote; but after that gentleman's administration ceased, where could they point out another so highly respected as to concentre a majority of ninety-one persons in his favor? and if no gentleman should be fully returned, then the government must stand still. He went over much of the ground which he had trod the preceding day, relative to the Eastern States[2] having been so guarded in what they had conceded to gain the regulation of our commerce, which threw into their hands the carrying trade, and put it in their power to lay us under payment of whatever freightage they thought proper to impose. It was their interest to do so, and no person could

2. New England

doubt but they would promote it by every means in their power. He wished our delegates had sufficiently attended to this point in the Convention—had been more attentive to this object, and taken care to have it expressed, in this Constitution, that all our ports were open to all nations; instead of putting us in the power of a set of men who may fritter away the value of our produce to a little or nothing, by compelling payment of exorbitant freightage. Neither did he believe it was in the power of the Eastern States to furnish a sufficient number of ships to carry our produce. It was, indeed, a general way of talking, that the Eastern States had a great number of seamen, a vast number of ships; but where were they? Why did they not come here now, when ships are greatly wanted? He should always wish to give them a preference, and so, no doubt, would many other gentlemen; and yet very few ships come here from the Eastern States. Another exceptionable point was, that we were to give up the power of taxing ourselves. During our connection with Great Britain, she left us the power of raising money in any way most convenient: a certain sum was only required to defray the public wants, but no mode of collecting it ever prescribed. In this new Constitution, every thing is transferred, not so much power being left us as Lord North offered to guaranty to us in his consiliatory plan. Look at the articles of union ratified between England and Scotland. How cautiously had the latter taken care of her interest in reserving all the forms of law—her representation in Parliament—the right of taxation—the management of her revenue—and all her local and municipal interests! Why take from us the right of paying our delegates, and pay them from the federal treasury? He remembered formerly what a flame was raised in Massachusetts, on account of Great Britain assuming the payment of salaries to judges and other state officers; and that this conduct was considered as originating in a design to destroy the independence of their government. Our local expenses had been nearly defrayed by our impost duty; but now that this was given away, and thrown into a general fund, for the use of all the states indiscriminately, we should be obliged to augment our taxes to carry on our local government, notwithstanding we were to pay a poll tax for our negroes. Paper money, too, was another article of restraint, and a popular point with many; but what evils had we ever experienced by issuing a little paper money to relieve ourselves from any exigency that pressed us? We had now a circulating medium which every body took. We used formerly to issue paper bills every year, and recall them every five, with great convenience and advantage. Had not paper money carried us triumphantly through the war, extricated us from difficulties generally supposed to be insurmountable, and fully established us in our independence? and now every thing is so changed that an entire stop must be put to any more paper emissions, however great our distress may be. It was true, no article of the Constitution declared there should not be jury trials in civil cases; yet this must be implied, because it stated that all crimes, except in cases of impeachment, shall be tried by a jury. But even if trials by jury were allowed, could any person rest satisfied with a mode of trial which prevents the parties from being obliged to bring a cause for discussion before a jury of men chosen from the vicinage, in a manner conformable to the present administration of justice, which had stood the test of time and experience, and ever been highly approved of? Mr. Lowndes expatiated some time on the nature of compacts, the sacred light in which they were held by all nations, and solemnly called on the house to consider whether it would not be better to add strength to the old Confederation, instead of hastily adopting another; asking whether a man could be looked on as wise, who, possessing a magnificent building, upon discovering a flaw, instead of repairing the injury, should pull it down, and build another. Indeed, he could not understand with what propriety the Convention proceeded to change the Confederation; for every person with whom he had conversed on this subject concurred in opinion that the sole object of appointing a convention was to inquire what alterations were necessary in the Confederation, in order that it might answer those salutary purposes for which it was originally intended.

He recommended that another convention should be called; and as the general sense of America appeared now to be known, every objection could be met on fair grounds, and adequate remedies applied where necessary. This mode of proceeding would conciliate all parties, because it was candid, and had a more obvious tendency to do away all inconveniences than the adoption of a government which perhaps might require the bayonet to enforce it; for it could not be expected that the people, who had disregarded the requisitions of Congress, though expressed in language the most elegant and forcible that he ever remembered to have read, would be more obedient to the government until an irresistible force compelled them to be so. Mr. Lowndes concluded a long speech with a glowing eulogy on the old Confederation, and challenged his opponents, whilst one state objected, to get over that section which said, "The Articles of this Confederation shall be inviolably observed in every state, and the Union shall be perpetual; nor shall any alteration at any time hereafter be made in them, unless such alteration be agreed to in a Congress of the United States, and be afterwards confirmed by the legislature of every state."

CHRONOLOGY

1754
The French and Indian War, the American portion of the Seven Years' War, begin.

1763
The French and Indian War ends with a British victory over the French.

1765
The Stamp Act is passed by Parliament; the Sons of Liberty is formed to protest the Stamp Act; the Stamp Act Congress declares "no taxation without representation."

1766
The Stamp Act is repealed by Parliament; the Declaratory Act is passed by Parliament, wherein it declares its authority to legislate for the colonies in all matters.

1767
The Townshend Acts are passed by Parliament.

1770
The Battle of Golden Hill takes place in New York City; the Townshend Acts are repealed by Parliament, except for the tax on tea; the Boston Massacre occurs.

1773
The Boston Tea Party takes place.

1775
The Battles at Lexington, Massachusetts, and Concord, New Hampshire, are fought; the Battle of Bunker Hill oc-

curs in Massachusetts; Americans invade Canada; the Battle of Great Bridge occurs in Virginia.

1776
The loyalists are defeated at the Battle of Moore's Creek in North Carolina; the British fail to capture Charleston, South Carolina; the Declaration of Independence is signed; the British drive the Continental army out of New York City; the Battle of Trenton is fought in New Jersey.

1777
The Battles of Princeton (New Jersey), Brandywine Creek (Pennsylvania), and Germantown (Pennsylvania) are fought; the British army general John Burgoyne surrenders at Saratoga, New York.

1778
France enters the war as America's ally; the Battle of Monmouth Courthouse occurs in New Jersey; Wyoming Valley (Pennsylvania) Massacre; George Rogers Clark captures Kaskaskia in the Ohio Territory; the British capture Savannah, Georgia; Cherry Valley (New York) Massacre.

1779
Clark captures Vincennes in the Ohio Territory; the British raid Virginia, burning Norfolk and Portsmouth.

1780
The British capture Charleston, South Carolina; the Battle of Camden is fought in South Carolina and the Battle of Kings Mountain in North Carolina.

1781
The Battles of Cowpens and Guilford Courthouse occur in North Carolina; the Articles of Confederation go into effect; the Battle of Yorktown is fought in Virginia.

1783
The Treaty of Paris ends the war.

1787
The Constitutional Convention draws up the U.S. Constitution.

1789
President George Washington and the First Congress take office.

1791
The Bill of Rights goes into effect.

FOR FURTHER RESEARCH

Bernard Bailyn, *The Ideological Origins of the American Revolution*. Cambridge, MA: Belknap Press of Harvard University Press, 1992.

Ian Barnes and Charles Royster, eds., *The Historical Atlas of the American Revolution*. New York: Routledge, 2000.

Walter H. Blumenthal, *Women Camp Followers of the American Revolution*. New York: Arno, 1974.

Colin Bonwick, *The American Revolution*. Charlottesville: University Press of Virginia, 1991.

Richard D. Brown, ed., *Major Problems in the Era of the American Revolution, 1760–1791*. Boston: Houghton Mifflin, 2000.

Colin G. Calloway, *The American Revolution in Indian Country: Crisis and Diversity in Native American Communities*. New York: Cambridge University Press, 1995.

Henry Steele Commager and Richard B. Morris, eds., *The Spirit of 'Seventy-Six: The Story of the American Revolution as Told by Participants*. New York: Harper & Row, 1967.

Jonathan R. Dull, *A Diplomatic History of the American Revolution*. New Haven, CT: Yale University Press, 1985.

Sylvia R. Frey, *Water from the Rock: Black Resistance in a Revolutionary Age*. Princeton, NJ: Princeton University Press, 1991.

Jack P. Greene and J.R. Pole, eds., *The Blackwell Encyclopedia of the American Revolution*. Cambridge, MA: Blackwell, 1991.

Don Higginbotham, *The War of American Independence: Military Attitudes, Policies, and Practice, 1763–1789.* Boston: Northeastern University Press, 1983.

Mark V. Kwasny, *Washington's Partisan War, 1775–1783.* Kent, OH: Kent State University Press, 1996.

Piers Mackesy, *The War for America, 1775–1783.* Lincoln: University of Nebraska Press, 1993.

Daniel Marston, *The American Revolution, 1774–1783.* Oxford, England: Osprey, 2002.

Michael Pearson, *Those Damned Rebels: The American Revolution as Seen Through British Eyes.* New York: G.P. Putnam's Sons, 1972.

Benjamin Quarles, *The Negro in the American Revolution.* Chapel Hill: University of North Carolina Press, 1961.

Paul H. Smith, *Loyalists and Redcoats: A Study in British Revolutionary Policy.* Chapel Hill: University of North Carolina Press, 1964.

Barbara W. Tuchman, *The First Salute: A View of the American Revolution.* New York: Ballantine Books, 1988.

Christopher Ward, *The War of the American Revolution.* 2 vols. Ed. John R. Alden. New York: Macmillan, 1952.

Gordon S. Wood, *The Creation of the American Republic, 1776–1787.* Chapel Hill: University of North Carolina Press, 1998.

———, *The Radicalism of the American Revolution.* New York: Vintage Books, 1993.

INDEX

American colonies
  ability of, to handle local
    affairs, 13
  are not exempt from
    British taxation, 44–45
  are not represented in
    Parliament, 47–48
  British sympathy with,
    82–83
  desire for constitution of,
    65–66
  duty of, to pay taxes,
    62–63
  financing the war and,
    22–23, 102–105
  Great Britain's authority
    over, 66–68
  ideas of, about
    government, 14–15
  independence of, from
    Great Britain
    argument for, 53–56
    declaration of, 61–62
    would ruin the British
      Empire, 60–61
  legislative powers in, 60,
    64–65
  must be dependent on
    Great Britain, 59–60
  patriot vs. loyalist militias
    in, 19
  reaction of, to Stamp Act,
    15–16, 36
  sound parts of, 83–84
  on virtual representation,
    16–17, 36
  voting rights of, 50
  see also civilians;
    Continental army; states
American Revolution
  (1775–1781)
  colonists' efforts to
    prevent, 54–55
  end of, 30
  Englishman's call for end
    to, 84–85
  events of
    1775, 23–24
    1776, 24–25
    1777, 25–26
    1778, 26–28
    1779, 28
    1780, 28–29
    1781, 29–30
  financing of, 102–105
  as inevitable, 56
  major battles of, 27
  obstacles to winning,
    19–20
  reasons for, 13
  see also British army;
    Continental army
anti-federalists, 161
armies. *See* British army;
  Continental army
Arnold, Benedict, 25
Articles of Confederation,
  160

hunger of, 116, 132–33
lifestyle of, while lodging
with civilians, 123–30
Thanksgiving celebration
of, 113–14
thirst of, 115–16
waiting of, for relief, 110
wounded, 134, 135
see also Continental army
Sons of Liberty, 16
South Carolina, 30–31
Southern Expedition, 25
Spain, threat of naval force
from, 90–92
Stamp Act (1765)
American reaction to,
15–16, 36
purpose of, 15, 36
repeal of, 16
representation and, 47–48
Stamp Act Congress'
grievances on, 38–40
Stamp Act Congress
(1765), 16, 37
state constitutions, 160
states
Articles of Confederation
as a threat to, 32
Continental Congress vs.
governments of, 31–32
creation of governments
of, 30–31
support for powers of,
191
see also Articles of
Confederation
Stone, Joel, 139
Stone, William T., 131

taxation
American colonies are not
exempt from, 44–45
Articles of Confederation
and, 195–96
British non-electors and,
49
consent of individual and,
42–43
criticism of a strong
national government on,
192, 206–207
financing the war and, 22,
103–104
right of British Empire
over, 42, 62–63
see also Stamp Act (1765)
Tea Act (1773), 17
Tories. See loyalists
trade
Articles of Confederation
and, 33
congressional power over,
186–88
criticism of federal powers
on, 205–206
national vs. state powers
over, 198
Royal Navy and, 87–88

U.S. Constitution
altering Articles of
Confederation vs. a new,
207–208
convention for, 33–34
creation of, 160, 161
debate over, 161
ratification of, 34

reasons for, 32–33

Virginia
Bill of Rights of, 163–65
constitution of, 30–31,
165–73
virtual representation
American colonists and,
48–51
American response to,
16–17, 36
British Parliament
member on, 43–44
British proposition for, 16,
36
voting. *See* elections;
representation

Washington, George,
24–25, 29–30, 93
Wister, Sarah, 119
women
bringing water to soldiers,
135
camping with soldiers,
132
during surrender of
Burgoyne's campaign,
136–38
helping the wounded, 135
influenced by the war, 107
preparing food, 132–33
staying in cellars with
soldiers, 133
worrying about husbands,
135–36